NG PLACES OF INTEREST

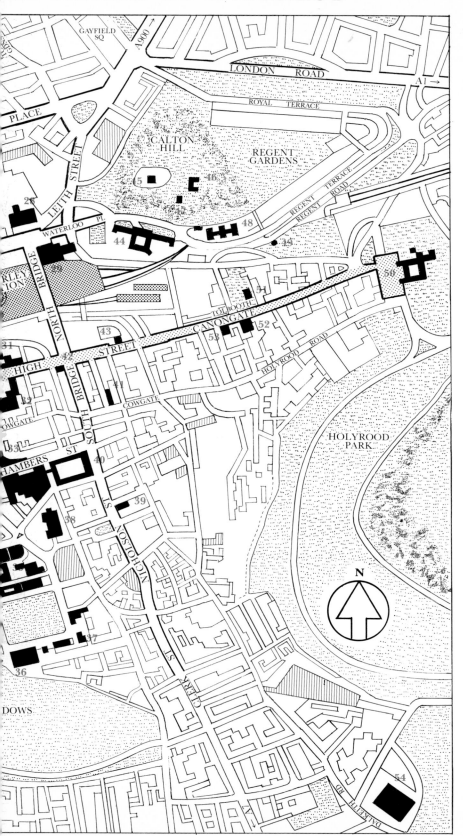

Key

1. St Mary's Episcopal Cathedral
2. West Register House
3. St John's Episcopal Church
4. St Cuthbert's Church
5. Lyceum Theatre
6. Argyle House
7. Castle
8. Scottish American War Memorial
9. Freemasons' Hall
10. St Stephen's Church
11. Assembly Rooms
12. Royal Scottish Academy
13. National Gallery
14. Ramsay Gardens
15. New College
16. Lady Stair's House
17. Tolbooth St John's
18. College of Art
19. George Heriot's Hospital School
20. Royal Infirmary
21. Greyfriars Church
22. St Giles' Cathedral
23. Sheriff's Court
24. Scott Monument
25. St Andrew's Church
26. National Portrait Gallery
27. Royal Bank of Scotland
28. Register House
29. General Post Office
30. Tourist Information
31. City Chambers
32. Parliament House
33. Heriot Watt University
34. Royal Scottish Museum
35. University Medical Faculty
36. University Library
37. David Hume Tower
38. Student Centre
39. Surgeons' Hall
40. University Old College
41. St Cecilia's Hall
42. Tron Kirk
43. John Knox's House
44. St Andrew's House
45. Observatory
46. National Monument
47. Nelson Monument
48. Royal High School Building
49. Burns Monument
50. Holyrood Palace
51. Canongate Church
52. Huntly House Museum
53. Moray House
54. Royal Commonwealth Pool

▦ Royal Mile

▨ Parking

EDINBURGH

EDINBURGH

Text by
MALCOLM MACDONALD

With photographs by
ERNEST FRANKL

THE PEVENSEY PRESS
Cambridge England

For my parents

Published by The Pevensey Press, 6 De Freville Ave, Cambridge CB4 1HR, UK

Photographs: Ernest Frankl, except 5, 50, 51: Malcolm MacDonald; 6, 20, 41, 59, 60, 64: Scottish Tourist Board; 37: Royal Scottish Museum; 57: Stephen Smith, Woodmansterne

Map: Carmen Frankl

Edited by Ruth Smith

Design by Kate Hughes-Stanton; design and production in association with Book Production Consultants, Cambridge

ISBN 0 907115 23 3 (hard covers); 0 907115 24 1 (paperback)

Typesetting in Baskerville by Westholme Graphics Ltd

Printed in Italy by Canale, Turin in association with Keats European.

Front cover Edinburgh Castle on its basalt rock, seen against the sky from Johnstone Terrace to the south. Facing the viewer are the old Royal Apartments, birthplace of King James VI of Scotland (James I of England); part of the Half Moon Battery is visible on the right.

Frontispiece (**1**) Princes Street, seen from Calton Hill, is fenced by ranks of notable Edinburgh verticals. From left to right, the prominent towers are the North British Hotel's clock tower; the Scott Monument; St John's Church at the far end of Princes Street; St George's West Church in Shandwick Place; and the three spires of St Mary's Cathedral. The astrolabe on the right surmounts Burtons, a large Edwardian department store building.

Back cover The early-20th-century vaulted ceiling of the Thistle Chapel in St Giles' Cathedral. The chapel is the most ornate building of its kind erected in Scotland since the 15th century. The decoration was directly inspired by medieval examples; the bosses visible here carry the diagonal cross of St Andrew, patron saint of Scotland.

Contents

1 Dreams in Masonry and Living Rock

Edinburgh is the capital of Scotland; a site resonant with a thousand years of historical associations; a seat of government; a centre of learning, sport, and the arts; and for landscape and architecture one of the most spectacular cities of Europe. One of its politer epithets is 'the Athens of the North' – and like Athens it has an acropolis; like Salzburg, it is dominated by a medieval castle on a towering crag; like Rome, it straddles a system of seven hills, but they easily outshine Rome's for size and grandeur. Indeed Edinburgh presents almost a surfeit of spectacle, so that for many people it has a strangely unreal quality. To Robert Haydon, visiting Sir Walter Scott in Hanover Street in 1820, it was 'the dream of a great genius'. Robert Louis Stevenson, Edinburgh-born and bred, characterized it as a 'profusion of eccentricities, this dream in masonry and living rock', the more astonishing for being 'not a dropscene in a theatre, but a city in the world of everyday reality'.

The city owes everything to its geographical position, and to the prehistoric processes of fire and ice. The Lothian Basin, a fertile plain between Scotland's Southern Uplands and the great arm of the sea called the Firth of Forth, narrows with the northward advance of the Pentland Hills. Precisely here, between the Pentlands and the sea, a tight cluster of volcanoes reared up: Arthur's Seat, Salisbury Crags, Calton Hill, and the Castle Rock began life as its principal cones. Long after the fires had died, glaciers eroded the lava in an easterly direction, so that all these hills have a steep scarp facing west and a long dip-slope canting east. The former volcanoes, near the sea and surrounded by good farming land, provided a first-class defensive site in a highly strategic location: they lay athwart the principal route from the south into Scotland's Central Lowlands and to the Highlands beyond.

The Castle Rock (**7**), an isolated basalt plug 437 feet above sea level, was the original focus of settlement. The Romans had a hill-fort here when southern Scotland was the province of Valentia; doubtless they were not the first, and after their departure the Picts moved in, eventually establishing a village on the gentle eastern slope which seems to have been called *Dun-edin*, 'fortress on the ridge'. The Angles of Northumbria occupied the area in the 7th century, led by a King Edwin who rebuilt the fort and, in transposing the Gaelic name into Anglo-Saxon, had only to interpolate a *w* to make it *Edwinesburgh*.

The independent Scottish kingdom came into being through many tribulations and wars between Gaelic-speaking and Saxon-speaking factions in the 9th and 10th centuries, and after it was established Edinburgh was closely connected with the fortunes of its kings and queens. It was King Malcolm III

2 *A typical Edinburgh perspective of contrasting architectures, looking north from the Castle Esplanade to the Mounds, the Royal Scottish Academy, Princes Street, the roofs of the New Town with the spire of St Andrew's Church, modern tower blocks at Leith, and the Firth of Forth vanishing into the haze.*

Canmore (1057–93), conqueror of Macbeth and last of the purely Gaelic kings, who decided to make a royal residence out of the scatter of buildings on the summit of Castle Rock; and the chapel which he built for his Saxon queen (St Margaret, grand-niece of Edward the Confessor) is the oldest building that survives there today (**13**). The Scottish capital at this period was Dunfermline, across the water in Fife, but Edinburgh's strategic position demanded a fairly continuous royal presence. Malcolm's English-educated son David I (1124–49), who extended Scotland's border as far as the River Tees, built a small walled town immediately to the east of the castle, which gradually began to grow eastward and downhill along the slope in the direction of his other notable foundation, the Abbey of Holyrood.

The first Scottish Parliament was convened in Edinburgh in the reign of William the Lion (1165–1214), 70 years before such a gathering was held in England. Under the powerful King Alexander III (1249–86) the Castle came to house the national records and Scottish regalia. The disputed succession after Alexander's sudden death laid Scotland open to occupation by the English, which sparked off a bloody 30-year war of liberation, with Edinburgh changing hands several times. Robert the Bruce, a fugitive guerilla leader, finally shattered a huge English army at Bannockburn in 1314 and was recognised by the Pope as rightful King of Scotland in 1323. He held a Parliament at Holyrood and in 1329 granted a new charter to the city giving Edinburgh rights over the coastal village of Leith, whose importance as a trading harbour was beginning to be appreciated. Through this and other sea-routes Scotland kept its own lines of communication to the Continent, and throughout the Middle Ages France, rather than England, was the natural ally and influence.

4 *The 15th-century Moubray House has the outside staircase and timber gable characteristic of Old Town architecture. An early resident was the painter George Jamesone, a pupil of Rubens and a friend of Van Dyck. Since then the building has been a tavern, the bookshop of Sir Walter Scott's publisher Archibald Constable, and a temperance hotel; it is now privately occupied once more.*

3 *Arthur's Seat from the vicinity of Dunsappie Loch. Crow Hill, at the left, is part of the so-called Lion's Haunch Vent of the original Carboniferous Era volcano. Above it rises the summit, the Lion's Head.*

CRAFTS

TO 13 HIGH STREET
TRUNK'S CLOSE

The Edinburgh Woollen Mill

From King Robert's daughter descended the brilliant and ill-starred House of Stewart, with whose monarchs Edinburgh has been particularly associated. Aeneas Sylvius Piccolomini, the future Pope Paul II, visited the poet-King James I in Edinburgh Castle as papal ambassador. James II (1437–60) held his Parliaments regularly in the town, and it was probably during his reign that Edinburgh became *de facto* capital of Scotland. He was also responsible for turning the marshy hollow immediately north of Castle Rock into an artificial lake, the Nor' Loch, which remained a landmark and defensive barrier until the 18th century. His grandson James IV (1488–1513), who united the flair of a Renaissance prince with the pageantry of the late Middle Ages, began the building of the Palace of Holyroodhouse, established the Scottish Navy, founded the Royal College of Surgeons, encouraged the spread of education, and granted Chepman and Myllar the rights to set up the first printing-press in Scotland. It was in his time that the stretch of town between Holyrood and the Castle came to be called the Royal Mile, and it was along this route that the wedding procession moved when he married the English King Henry VII's daughter Margaret Tudor in 1503 and the public fountains ran with wine. But James' reign – and his statesmanlike attempts to preserve the peace of Europe – ended in disaster. Having been dragged into war by the 'Auld Alliance' when Henry VIII invaded France, he was defeated and slain with many of his nobles and burghers at the Battle of Flodden Field. Fear of an English invasion spurred the building of a new defensive wall around the city.

The troubled and melancholy James V (1513–42) established Edinburgh's Court of Session and continued the building of Holyroodhouse. His daughter Mary, Queen of Scots, was born only a few days before his death: during her minority, while her French mother, Mary of Guise, was Regent, the power-struggles of the nobility were aggravated by the religious strife of the Reformation. John Knox (1505–72), the fiery and extreme Calvinist preacher, became minister in Edinburgh in 1556, and clashed bitterly with the young Catholic queen, who had been married as a child to the Dauphin of France and returned to Scotland in 1561 for a brief, unhappy, and still controversial reign. For some, Mary is an archetypal figure of romance; for others, a political incompetent incapable of strong government in crucial times, in sad contrast to her cousin Elizabeth I of England. The Protestant party was victorious: in 1568 Mary was forced to escape to England, where (being a focus of opposition to Elizabeth) she was imprisoned and executed. But her son James VI, who founded Edinburgh's University, succeeded Elizabeth as James I of England in 1603, and henceforth the two kingdoms were united. The present British Royal Family descends directly from James' daughter Elizabeth, the 'Winter Queen' of Bohemia.

Although the court removed to London, Edinburgh remained the seat of Scotland's Parliament until 1707. As in England, the Civil War period was a prolongation and intensification of the religious conflicts of the previous century. The Presbyterian party had to fight Charles I's attempt to introduce an Episcopalian church hierarchy. Riots in St Giles' Cathedral led to rebellion and the declaration in 1638 of a National Covenant pledging support to a purely Presbyterian Church of Scotland. The Covenanters, roughly equivalent to the extreme Puritan party in England, endured fierce persecution and were fierce persecutors in their turn when opportunity allowed. The tides of war brought Oliver Cromwell to occupy the city in 1650, when much of Holyroodhouse was

5 *Looking south from Calton Hill: a panorama encompassing most of the Old Town, shimmering in a September heat haze. The Royal Mile sweeps eastward down the slope from the Castle, visible at the extreme right. The most prominent spires are (from right to left) those of Tolbooth St John's, St Giles' Cathedral, and the Tron Kirk.*

destroyed by fire. The Restoration of Charles II saw its rebuilding, and the future James VII (II of England) lived there for a time as Duke of York.

The Union of the Parliaments in 1707 was deeply unpopular in Scotland, and afterwards Edinburgh's political history was of local rather than national signficance – except for the Jacobite Rebellions of 1715 and 1745. During the '45 James VII's grandson Prince Charles Edward Stewart, 'the Young Pretender', held court at Holyrood and won a spectacular victory at the Battle of Prestonpans, just east of the city, before his ill-fated invasion of England.

Despite the Parliamentary Union Scotland retained (and retains) its own legal system, more closely related to Roman and French than to English Law. The 18th and early 19th centuries were a golden age of Edinburgh lawyers: the fearsome hanging judge Lord Braxfield; Duncan Forbes; Francis Jeffrey, who founded the *Edinburgh Review*; the Whig Solicitor-General Lord Henry Cockburn (1779–1854), architect of the 1832 Reform Bill in Scotland, who vividly recreated the age in *Memorials of His Time*; and the Tory Sir Walter Scott. As these names show, legal, political, and literary worlds overlapped; and the same period saw Edinburgh established as one of the most important cultural centres in Britain. Besides those already mentioned its denizens included the poets Allan Ramsay, Robert Fergusson, and Robert Burns; the poet and novelist James Hogg; the novelist Henry Mackenzie; the economist Adam Smith; the philosophers David Hume and Dugald Stewart; the painter Henry Raeburn; and the folk-music collector George Thomson, for whose tunes Burns wrote some of his best-known poems, while Haydn, Beethoven, and Weber provided the arrangements. Oliver Goldsmith studied medicine at the University; Dr Johnson, Smollett, Turner, and Stendahl were notable visitors.

This period of cultural expansion coincided with the physical expansion of the city. Edinburgh had so far remained a crowded medieval town strung along the narrow tail of the Castle Rock (**5**), but in the 1760s ambitious building projects initiated a new magnificence. The first growth was to the south, around George Square; but far vaster was the New Town of Edinburgh, a series of carefully controlled and highly imaginative developments to the north whose

11

streets, squares, crescents, and gardens increased the city's area tenfold during the next 70 years and endowed it with the most extensive Georgian and Regency urban architecture still surviving in the British Isles.

It was therefore a heroic age for architects as well, the most famous being Robert Adam (1728–92), a towering figure in the history of Neoclassicism, who designed some of his finest buildings for Edinburgh. Less well known outside Edinburgh, because he devoted so much of his energy to it, was William H. Playfair (1789–1857), who finished much that Adam had begun. You cannot walk far in the city without encountering a Playfair building or monument or even railway cutting; he put his signature to every skyline. Others who left their mark on the city were James Craig, who planned the first New Town, William Stark, who envisaged the Calton Hill scheme, William Burn, Thomas Hamilton, Robert Reid, and James Gillespie Graham, friend of Pugin and designer of the magnificent Moray Estate. Their combined talents gave Edinburgh much of its distinctive character, which modern developments have so far failed to efface.

The 1830s and 1840s saw the end of the New Town projects and brought the Industrial Revolution to Edinburgh in the shape of the railway, and coal-mining to its surrounding villages. Light industry expanded: the city is famous for printing, publishing, paper-making, and brewing, and also for the businesses of banking and insurance. The reputation of the University, especially its Faculty of Medicine, spread throughout the country. George IV's visit in 1822 was the first by a reigning monarch for over a century, and Holyroodhouse resumed its function as an occasional royal residence.

The modern town has added electronics and light engineering to its indus-

7 *Edinburgh Castle on its basalt rock, seen against the sky from Johnstone Terrace to the south. Facing the viewer are the old Royal Apartments, birthplace of King James VI of Scotland (James I of England); part of the Half Moon Battery is visible on the right.*

6 *The Military Tattoo is the most popular event of the annual Edinburgh International Festival, performed every night on the Esplanade against the dramatic backdrop of the Castle, and involving a different cast of British and Commonwealth participants each year.*

tries; enhanced its prestige as a shopping centre by opening the pedestrian precincts of Rose Street and the huge St James' Centre; and acquired a second university (Heriot Watt) and an important college of advanced education (Napier College). Over the past 40 years it has attracted a new international reputation as a centre for conferences and, especially, as the home of the Edinburgh International Festival.

Founded in 1947, the Festival is an annual three-week celebration of all the arts. Its primary emphasis is on music and the theatre, with visits of orchestras, soloists, and opera and drama companies from all over the world; but there are also always many art exhibitions, a concurrent Film Festival, and the spectacular Military Tattoo, which takes place nightly on the Castle Esplanade against the floodlit backdrop of the Castle (6). Quite as important is the Festival Fringe, to which as many as 800 professional and amateur companies contribute a gamut of 'unofficial' events in every branch of the arts – it has been called 'probably the largest cultural event on the planet'. Many of the numerous open-air and street theatre presentations find a congenial setting in Holyrood Park. Two perennial criticisms of the Festival are that Edinburgh people take little interest in it, and that it includes disproportionately little Scottish music and art; but it is a tremendous tourist attraction, and brings a vast amount of business to the city.

A festival could have no finer setting. The place itself, as Stevenson wrote, 'is full of theatre tricks in the way of scenery . . . you turn to the back window of a grimy tenement in a lane, and behold, you are face to face with distant and bright prospects. You turn a corner, and there is the sun going down into the Highland hills. You look down an alley, and see ships tacking for the Baltic.' The Baltic trade is not what it was, and the ships, being oil-fired, tack no longer; the city is possibly a little cleaner than in Stevenson's day. But it is essentially his Edinburgh, his theatrical 'dropscene', that awaits the visitor today. Function may change but the fabric remains. (The corner shop where Stevenson, as a boy, bought his toy theatres was a newsagent's in the present writer's childhood, and now houses an Italian restaurant.) Despite the inroads of modern planners, the restoration of the Old Town and the preservation of the New have left Edinburgh a city of bold, indeed dizzying contrasts. The Old Town is fundamentally a medieval and Renaissance creation; the New Town is almost purely Georgian, that is to say, Neoclassical: nowhere else in Britain can one find such an accumulation of imposing structures echoing the glories of Greece and Rome.

These strong, opposing architectures are in heroic competition with the landscape itself, for the topography the volcanoes and glaciers sculpted is too rugged to be obliterated by mere buildings. Edinburgh is rich in parks, in gardens, in avenues of trees; but also in hillsides and sheer basalt cliffs. The Old Town clings to the spine of the Castle Rock; the eastern portion of the New Town encloses Calton Hill; and in Holyrood Park, whose boundaries include Arthur's Seat and Salisbury Crags, the centre of Edinburgh has direct access to an authentic mountain wilderness.

Arthur's Seat (3, 51), the largest of Edinburgh's hills (822 feet above sea level), is most probably named after Arthur, Prince of Strathclyde (508–42) – and not, as often thought, after the King Arthur of legend. From certain viewpoints (such as Meadowbank to the north or Newington to the south) Arthur's Seat and Salisbury Crags together form the outline of a gigantic lion

8 *The early-20th-century vaulted ceiling of the Thistle Chapel, the most ornate building of its kind erected in Scotland since the 15th century. The decoration was directly inspired by medieval examples; the bosses visible here carry the diagonal cross of St Andrew, patron saint of Scotland.*

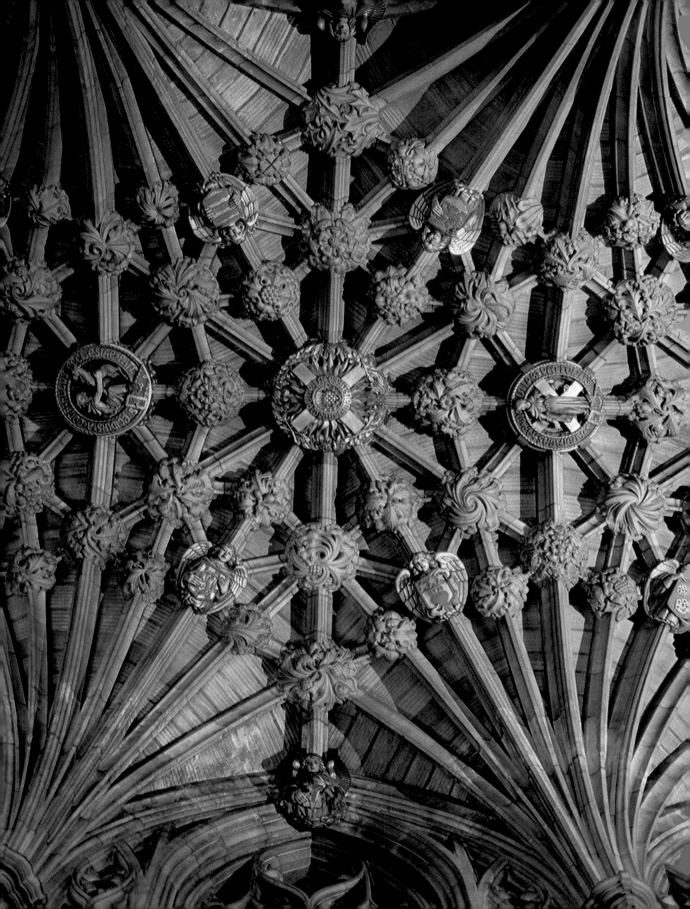

couchant, with the Crags its huge paws and the summit of Arthur's Seat its raised, alert head. From the summit – a popular climb, and easier than it looks – you have the most panoramic view of Edinburgh and (visibility permitting) its situation in relation to the rest of Scotland: the Pentland Hills to the south, the Central Lowland plain to the west, and to the north and north-west the Firth, Fife, and the peaks of the Highland massif 70 or 80 miles distant. Here May Day is still observed with a sunrise service, and occasionally druidic rites, and it was here that James Hogg placed the terrifying battle between good and evil in one of the most remarkable of all Scottish novels, *The Confessions of a Justified Sinner* (1813).

Descending, you are surrounded by clefts and valleys, and the city is hidden from view. Flocks of sheep crop the grass, moving among the hills. By the foot of **Salisbury Crags** winds the picturesque Radical Road, built in 1820 and so called because its construction was entrusted, at Sir Walter Scott's suggestion, to a group of unemployed weavers from the west who were believed to harbour 'radical' political tendencies. There are three lochs within the park. **St Margaret's Loch** is little more than an artificial pond, overlooked by the 15th-century **St Anthony's Chapel**, a ruin believed to date from the reign of James I. **Dunsappie Loch**, deep and isolated within the hills, is evocatively mysterious. **Duddingston Loch**, the largest, is on the south side of Arthur's Seat and is a sanctuary for waterfowl. Adjoining it is **Duddingston Village**, originally a weaving settlement and typical of the many once-outlying communities which have become characterful suburbs. It has an attractive 12th-century church (with many additions of the 17th–19th centuries), and just to

9 *George Square was designed and built in the 1760s by James Brown as a private speculation, and long after the New Town was established it remained a fashionable residential area. Though much of the original housing has disappeared, leaving it a preserve of the modern University, this view across its central gardens gives some idea of its original grace and scale.*

the east is **Duddingston House** (now a motel), an austere two-storey villa with Corinthian portico, built for the architect Sir William Chambers in 1768. Adjacent to the house, **Duddingston Golf Course** is one of the best in the city – which is saying much, for Edinburgh, 'the golfing capital of the world', has 22 courses within its boundaries. Scots thrift has found a use for many of the city's wild green expanses, as fairways.

Sport of all kinds is important to Edinburgh, which has two League Football teams (Hibernian and Heart of Midlothian) and one of the world's great international rugby grounds at **Murrayfield**. Murrayfield also has an ice-rink; there is motor-racing to the west of the city at **Ingliston** and horse-racing at Musselburgh race-course to the east; and **Hillend**, in the south, boasts the largest artificial ski-slope in Britain. Just to the north of Holyrood Park is **Meadowbank Sports Stadium**, a 15,000-seat complex under a vast canti-levered steel roof, opened in 1970 as the venue for that year's Commonwealth Games. The **Royal Commonwealth Swimming Pool**, built for the same event, contains three pools, one to Olympic standard: it lies on the opposite side of Arthur's Seat, its clean horizontal lines contrasting with the brooding hill-sides. Almost next door are two more of Edinburgh's relatively few really striking modern buildings, the Swedish-style **Pollock Halls of Residence** for the University, and the **Scottish Widows Assurance Headquarters** (1976), designed by Sir Basil Spence. To stand in Dalkeith Road and lift one's eyes from its dark glass hexagons to the hills beyond is to see the confrontation of primeval and contemporary Edinburgh at its most theatrical.

10 *The Argyll Battery, above the Argyll Tower, is the setting for a display of cannon; beyond is a distant vista westward towards the Forth Bridges.*

2 The Old Town

One building dominates Edinburgh's skyline more than any other: **Edinburgh Castle** (**7**). Its dominance is wholly appropriate, since it was the first part of the area to be settled – the defensive kernel from which the city began to grow. Turreted and battlemented on its precipitous crag, the Castle offers dramatic aspects from many vantage points. The classic view is of its north side, from Princes Street, which parallels the crag's east–west alignment; from the Mound one may study its wooded and relatively gentle eastern slopes (**12**); on the south side the Grassmarket affords an unrivalled impression of grey walls looming above a cliff-face; while the western end, anchored to the brow of the scarp, is best appreciated from St Cuthbert's churchyard. It is a commanding and almost impregnable situation. Since 1296, when the invading King Edward I of England reduced the defences with artillery and installed his own garrison, the Castle has only once been taken – and then by stealth. That was the celebrated occasion in 1314 when Sir Thomas Randolph, Earl of Moray, scaled the north face of the rock with 30 men to drive out the English and restore the Castle to King Robert the Bruce. Since then the Castle has withstood many sieges – the longest from 1570 to 1573 when Kirkaldy of Grange defended it against the enemies of Mary, Queen of Scots; the last in 1689, when the Duke of Gordon held out for James VII (James II of England). It still houses a small military detachment.

The Castle must be approached from the east, through the **Esplanade** constructed in the 19th century as a parade ground, and now the setting for the famous Military Tattoo during the Festival (see above, p. 14). It is also an excellent viewpoint for the south side of the city. The Esplanade walls bear many memorial plaques to members of Scottish regiments who fell overseas. A small bronze well in the north-east corner (furthest from the Castle) marks the spot on which over 300 Edinburgh women were burned at the stake as witches between 1479 and 1722. Nearest to the Castle a small area of ground is officially Canadian territory, by virtue of an Act of Charles I, enabling the selling of baronetcies to prospective settlers in Nova Scotia, which required that the buyer be given a token portion of soil. The Castle itself is entered by a drawbridge over a dry fosse, into the 16th-century Morton's Gateway, an archway flanked by guardhouses. On either side of the main gate are modern statues – of Sir William Wallace (1270–1305), leader of the national resistance against Edward I's invasion, who was barbarously executed in London after his capture by the English; and of Robert the Bruce (1274–1329), who continued the struggle, became King of Scotland, and dealt Edward II a devastating

11 *The Argyll Tower spans the roadway into the Castle just above Morton's Gateway. First erected in 1574, it used to be the State Prison, and the Marquis of Argyll was incarcerated here before his execution in 1685. The archway once contained a gate and portcullis. The central shield on the tower was defaced by Cromwell, and later restored by Nelson the publisher.*

19

defeat at the Battle of Bannockburn in 1314. Sadly, the figures are pure products of imagination, as no reliable representation of either man exists.

The main path through the Castle winds in a snaking spiral, climbing steeply from the gate to the **Argyll Battery** (**10**), which has a fine display of cannon and affords a spectacular panorama of Princes Street, the New Town, the Firth of Forth, and – depending on the clearness of the day – the Fife coast and the Lomond Hills. On the south side of the Battery is the French prison, where captives taken during the Napoleonic Wars were held, as R. L. Stevenson describes in *St Ives*. Here stands 'Mons Meg', a bulky iron bombard variously reputed to have been forged in Flanders or in the Castle itself in the reign of James IV (1488–1513). In prime condition she had a range of nearly a mile and a half, and was used for salutes on royal occasions, such as Mary, Queen of Scots' engagement to the Dauphin of France. Installed in the Tower of London from 1759 to 1829, Meg was returned to the Castle at the urging of Sir Walter Scott. The Castle's modern artillery still gives royal salutes, and at 1 p.m. sharp, every weekday since 1851, the 'One-o'-clock gun' has been fired from the Mills Mount Battery as a time-check for the citizens of Edinburgh.

The bulk of the buildings to be seen within the Castle walls are 17th century or later, but a further turn of the spiral roadway, through Foog's Gate, brings us to the summit of the Castle Rock and the Castle's oldest building – indeed the oldest building still in use in Edinburgh. This is **St Margaret's Chapel** (**13**), a small, simple Norman building of austere charm, dating from around 1076 and built for the Saint, a Saxon princess who fled to Scotland after the Norman Conquest, married King Malcolm III Canmore, and did much to encourage learning in her half-barbarian adopted realm. Adjacent to the Chapel is the

13 *The interior of St Margaret's Chapel, the Castle's oldest building, showing the beautiful ornamented Norman chancel arch.*

12 *The eastern end of the Castle from the Mound; the Argyll Tower is seen end-on, right of centre in this view. The upper curtain wall is pierced by the gunports of the Mills Mount Battery; the chapel-like building top left is the Scottish National War Memorial.*

Half Moon Battery, another grand vantage point, built by Regent Morton in 1574 after the large 14th-century tower of King David II was destroyed in the long siege.

South of the Chapel lie the buildings of **Palace Yard**, clustered around a square that is entered from its north-east corner at the end of the spiral roadway. The Palace itself, or King's Lodging, dates from the 16th century. Over its main doorway is a cipher of the initials of Mary, Queen of Scots and her worthless husband Henry Stewart, Lord Darnley. In 1566 Mary gave birth to the future James VI (destined to become James I of England) in a tiny room that overlooks the sheer drop of the southern crag. There is a persistent but unprovable rumour that her child was stillborn, and the newborn baby of a serving maid substituted. James VI himself extended the Palace block in 1615, building the stone-vaulted **Crown Room** where the 'Honours of Scotland' are displayed – the royal crown, the sceptre, and the sword of state. The crown is reputed to contain the circlet of gold with which Robert Bruce was crowned at Scone in 1306, but in its present form it dates from 1540 when it was remade, probably by French workmen, for King James V. The gold in it is certainly Scottish, as are some of its 94 pearls. The sceptre was bestowed on James IV by the Borgia Pope Alexander VI (and was also remodelled for James V); and Pope Julius II presented the sword of state to James IV in 1507.

James IV's **Great Hall**, once the seat of the Scottish Parliament and later used for state banquets, occupies the south side of the square; an exhibition of arms and armour is housed here. The west side is an old barracks which now contains the **Scottish United Services Museum**. On the north side stands the impressive **Scottish National Memorial** for the soldiers killed in the Great War, a stately neo-Gothic Hall of Honour designed by Sir Robert Lorimer and inaugurated in 1927. It occupies the site of a chapel founded by King David I in the early 12th century.

From the Castle to Parliament Square

Returning to the Castle Gate and crossing the Esplanade, the visitor is confronted by a great broad street, lined with high buildings, that descends almost due east. This is the famous **Royal Mile**, axis and chief artery of the medieval and Renaissance town, which gradually extruded itself from the Castle Rock, along the spine of the long dip slope, down to the Abbey of Holyrood a mile away in the valley bottom. Properly speaking the Mile is a continuous system of five streets, Castle Hill, the Lawnmarket, High Street, Canongate, and Abbey Strand, and on either side of them is the densest accumulation of historical associations in the city. Other streets join the Mile at right angles, and between these are literally scores of narrow closes and wynds – distinctive elements of Old Town architecture. A close provides entrance to a 'land' or tenement block (occasionally still with an external staircase) and sometimes to a 'court' (courtyard) behind it; in origin closes were the gardens (enclosures) of private homes, but as storey after storey was added to each house to accommodate the growing population they became mere passageways (**21**). Wynds are narrow and winding alleyways, thoroughfares open at either end; those on the north side of the Lawnmarket and High Street are often precipitous, some with descending stairways that always spiral to the left (to give advantage to the sword-arm of a defender).

14 *A typical section of Ramsay Gardens, the striking block of flats adjacent to the Esplanade. It originated in an unusual octagonal dwelling built by Allan Ramsay, which was popularly referred to as 'Goose-pie House'. The block was renovated in the 1890s with a view to attracting University staff to live in the Old Town.*

15 *The hexagonal stair tower of Lady Stair's House stands out from the characteristic shadow patterns of an Edinburgh close. Built by Sir William Gray of Pittendrum, the house was sold to his grand-daughter, the Dowager Countess of Stair, in 1719.*

16 *The great width of St Giles' is noticeable in this view of its western end. The West Door itself was completed in 1884; the tower and crown (1495) is the only portion of the medieval cathedral visible from outside, surmounted by a gold weathercock that has been in position since the 16th century. The cobbled expanse of Parliament Square was occupied by Edinburgh's Tolbooth until 1817.*

This honeycomb of side-alleys, many of them the scene of historic events, help to make the Royal Mile one of the most fascinating ancient streets in the world. But only in the past century has it become clean, picturesque, and respectable. In earlier times it was a foul, fetid, overcrowded slum, and the closes and wynds were bywords for filth and squalor. Refuse and night soil were thrown out of the tenement windows onto the street, and onto the passers-by, with only the traditional warning of 'Gardyloo!' (French *garde à l'eau*). The 'evening effluvia' caused Dr Johnson, stumping up the High Street, to hiss in Boswell's ear 'I smell *you* in the dark!' – encompassing in 'you' the whole Scottish nation. Not surprisingly the Old Town was highly vulnerable to plague, and the last cholera epidemic was as recent as 1849. At that date there were still reputedly 52 brothels between Castle Hill and the top of the Canongate, a distance so short that, with the Kirk (St Giles' Cathedral) and the Courts and the Parliament in their midst, there can have been little room for anything else.

To the left, as the visitor leaves the Esplanade for Castle Hill, is a striking if somewhat bizarre block of flats complete with towers and turrets – **Ramsay Gardens** (**14**), which has grown around an original octagonal dwelling built in the 18th century by the poet Allan Ramsay. The main structure is fanciful 19th-century neo-medieval accretion designed by Sir Patrick Geddes (1854– 1932), an enthusiastic pioneer of architectural conservation and town planning. The relatively excellent state of preservation of the Royal Mile is his most impressive monument. It was Geddes who took over the castellated **Outlook Tower**, a little further down on the left, and converted it to a museum. Originally the town house of the Laird of Cockpen (made famous in song by

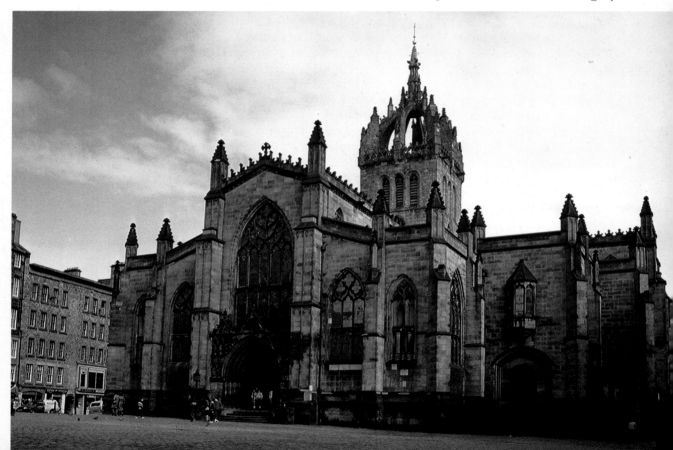

Lady Nairne), it had been extended upward in the 1850s by an optician, Maria Theresa Short, who set up a Camera Obscura in the hexagonal tower. The device is still in operating with improved lens and mirrors, throwing mysterious, silently moving images of Edinburgh across its tabletop screen.

Castle Hill begins at the junction on the south side with Castle Wynd; and on this corner stands **Canonball House**, a fine four-storey merchant's dwelling dated 1630. The cannonball lodged in the west wall is popularly supposed to have been fired from the Castle during the '45 rebellion, but in fact marks the high water level of Comiston Reservoir (several miles south near the Braid Hills), which started supplying water to Castle Hill's own reservoir in 1681. Further down, opposite Outlook Tower, are **Boswell's Court** (a tenement named after an uncle of Dr Johnson's friend) and the church of **Tolbooth St John** (the Tolbooth Kirk). This impressive example of Victorian Gothic was jointly designed by Pugin and James Gillespie Graham (they became friends after being shipwrecked together near Leith), to house the General Assembly of the Church of Scotland. Its pinnacled spire is the tallest in Edinburgh, and the interior contains excellent woodcarving, also designed by Pugin. The General Assembly moved to the other side of the street in the late 1850s, into **New College and Assembly Hall**, designed by William Playfair – uncharacteristically for him in neo-Gothic vein, and not quite confident enough to dominate the soaring tenement blocks that frame it. Nevertheless the College front, which looks northward away from Castle Hill to the Mound, is a pleasing piece of fantasy, especially when its tall gate-towers are seen framing the even taller spire of the Tolbooth Kirk behind. The building stands on the site of the 16th-century Palace of Mary of Guise and is often used for theatrical performances during the Festival.

The Tolbooth Kirk and College mark the top of the **Lawnmarket**, named after the old linen market. Immediately downhill from the Assembly Hall is **Milne's Court**, built in 1690 by Robert Mylne, who did much of the work on Holyrood Palace, and excellently renovated in 1971. Then comes **James Court**, where the philosopher David Hume lived and where Boswell entertained Dr Johnson in 1773. Next is **Gladstone's Land**, a romantically medieval-looking six-storey tenement that dates from 1550 but was remodelled in the early 17th century by the merchant Thomas Gledstanes, and is now open to the public under the aegis of the National Trust for Scotland. **Lady Stair's Close**, further down, contains Lady Stair's House (**15**, 1622), restored in pseudo-medieval style according to the ideas of Patrick Geddes, and now a literary museum to Robert Burns, Sir Walter Scott, and R. L. Stevenson. Opposite Gladstone's Land is **Riddle's Court**, another residence of David Hume, in which stands the late-16th-century house of the luckless Bailie McMorran, shot dead by pupils of the Royal High School when they rioted in 1595 against a reduction in school holidays. Further downhill on this side is **Brodie's Close**, named after the father of one of Edinburgh's most famous criminal hypocrites – Deacon Brodie. He was a pillar of the community by day and burglar by night, and was hanged in 1788. Robert Louis Stevenson collaborated with W. E. Henley on a play about him, and found in his character the inspiration for *Dr Jekyll and Mr Hyde*. Just east of here the Lawnmarket ends, crossed by George IV Bridge; we enter the **High Street**, and the area of St Giles'.

St Giles' Cathedral (**16**), the mother church of Presbyterianism, is dedicated to a 6th-century hermit whose cult is centred on Arles: the patron saint

17 *Most of the stained glass in St Giles' dates from the 19th century, when the cathedral was restored and partitioning walls were removed; by this time the Scottish Reformed Church had softened its attitude to the arts. The gable window on the north side is by William Morris and Sir Edward Burne-Jones (1886). The upper panels depict the Crossing of the Jordan, the lower contain the figures of Ruth, Miriam, and Jephtha's daughter.*

not only of Edinburgh but of cripples, lepers, tramps, and blacksmiths. (A reputed arm-bone of the saint was seized and thrown into the Nor' Loch by an iconoclastic mob in 1557). Charles I called the High Kirk a cathedral when he introduced bishops into the Church of Scotland, and the name stuck even after Presbyterianism was re-established by the 'Glorious Revolution' of 1688. The building is rather small for a cathedral, a compact yet massive Gothic structure, almost square in effect owing to its accumulation of chapels and aisles, and with a characteristically Scottish crowned tower instead of a spire. The fabric is essentially late 14th century, though the four huge octagonal pillars which bear the weight of the central tower are believed to survive from the previous Norman church, built in 1120 and razed by English invaders in 1385; even before that there was a religious foundation here, erected by monks from Holy Isle in 845. However, the facing, inside and out, is largely Victorian, as is almost all the stained glass (**17**).

The High Kirk has had a colourful history ever since medieval times (when the Scottish Parliament met in it). The poet Gavin Douglas, Chancellor of Scotland in 1514 and author of the great Scots translation of the *Aeneid*, was its provost. During the Reformation John Knox preached from one of its pulpits as First Minister of Edinburgh. Around the turn of the 16th century it was divided up and separate areas were used as law courts, the town clerk's office, a school, and a prison; the city gallows, including the prototype guillotine known as 'The Maiden' (now in the National Museum of Antiquities), were also stored in the building. When the Cathedral did return to purely religious functions, it was partitioned into four independent churches, each serving a different congregation, and was not reunified until its Victorian restoration in 1883.

18 *The Charles II statue in Parliament Square, seen against the background of the south side of St Giles'. Of Dutch manufacture, it is the only known equestrian statue of this king. One tradition insists that it was intended as a statue of Oliver Cromwell, but was given a new head after the Restoration.*

From about 1460 until they were demolished in the early 19th century, a group of timber-framed tenements, the Luckenbooths (locked booths), ran parallel with the Cathedral along its northern side; retailers set up stalls to sell fancy goods in the narrow intervening passageway (and in 1726 Allan Ramsay opened the first circulating library in Scotland in the first floor of the easternmost building).

The religious troubles prior to the Civil War inspired Jenny Geddes, a stallholder in the Luckenbooths, to become St Giles' most celebrated protestor against episcopacy. On 23 July 1637, hearing the recently installed bishop instruct the Dean to read the prayer for the day from the English prayer book, she yelled (according to tradition): 'False thief, will ye say mass about my lug?', or (according to contemporary report): 'De'il colic the wame o' ye', and launched her folding stool at the bishop's head. A plaque marks the spot where it hit, and records the riot that ensued. The end result of such disturbances was the National Covenant of 1638, establishing the Presbyterian Church of Scotland in defiance of Charles I. During the Civil War many Covenanters were imprisoned in the Cathedral; and the two greatest and bitterest adversaries in the Scottish theatre of the war, the royalist Marquis of Montrose and the covenanting Marquis of Argyll (whose 19th-century tombs face each other from opposite aisles of the Cathedral) were both executed within its shadow. Montrose was hanged at the Mercat Cross and Argyll was beheaded by 'The Maiden' before the West Door, on the roof of the city Tolbooth, which was demolished in 1817 (its groundplan is traced by brass plates inset into the cobbles next to St Giles'); a heart-shaped cobblestone design marks the Tolbooth's entrance and recalls its literary fame as the setting for the opening chapter of Scott's novel *Heart of Midlothian*.

19 *Parliament Square from the West Door of St Giles', facing the Lothian Regional Chambers: this building was called 'County Hall' when first erected (1816–18), and its design is based on one of the lesser temples of the Athenian Acropolis. In reconstructions at the turn of the century it was extended to join the Signet Library on the left.*

Of the additions to the Cathedral since its restoration the most gorgeous is the **Thistle Chapel** (8), the Chapel of the Most Ancient and Most Noble Order of the Thistle (Scotland's foremost order of chivalry), designed by Sir Robert Lorimer and completed in 1911. Its elaborate ornamentation and finely executed carvings include charming animal figures in the seats and angels playing musical instruments, the bagpipes among them. Above the Cathedral's west door is a memorial window to the poet Robert Burns (1985).

Behind the Cathedral, in **Parliament Square**, stands a lead equestrian statue, thought to be the oldest in Britain, of Charles II (18); and near it a flat stone with the legend 'I.K.1572' marks the reputed burial-place of John Knox. At the Square's entrance from the High Street is the **Mercat Cross**, from which royal proclamations are read. Part of the original 15th-century cross (demolished in 1756) remains in the shaft of the present cross, a modern replica set in an octagonal platform, erected by order of W. E. Gladstone while he was Prime Minister.

The principal buildings of Parliament Square are Edinburgh District Court and Court of Session (where Sir Walter Scott practised as an advocate), **Parliament House**, and the Signet Library. The Parliament House was the meeting place of the Scots Parliament between 1639 and the Union of 1707. Its exterior is undistinguished 19th-century work, but the upper of the two superimposed halls is the magnificent Parliament Hall, over 120 feet long and surmounted by a wonderful hammerbeam roof, constructed about 1640 (20). Notable among the fine collection of portraits and statuary it now houses is a

21 *Advocates Close, on the north side of the High Street, is named after Sir James Stewart of Goodtrees, Lord Advocate of Scotland at the end of the 17th century, who had his house here. It has the narrowness and steepness typical of the Old Town closes. Note the Victorian lamp, designed for gas light. The arch frames the upper half of the Scott Monument in East Princes Street Gardens.*

20 *Parliament Hall, with its splendid oak hammerbeam roof, was designed by John Scott in 1640 and is among the most impressive buildings of the flowering of Scottish architecture in the late 16th and early 17th centuries.*

superb statue by Roubiliac of one of Scotland's great lawyers, Duncan Forbes of Culloden (1685–1748), 'manager' of the Highlands for the Government after the failure of the '45 rebellion. Leaning forward in his seat, in the robes of Lord President of the Court of Session, Forbes is portrayed as the very archetype of the Scottish Judge – patriarchal, infallible, his outstretched hand dispensing law unanswerably. (There is a similar portrayal of the type in R. L. Stevenson's *Weir of Hermiston*.) The **Signet Library** houses numerous rare legal books and documents, and is the centre for the Society of Her Majesty's Writers to the Signet, an organization that dates back to 1600 and originated in the 15th-century keepers of the King's Seal, or signet; by the mid-18th century it had grown to constitute the principal order of solicitors in Scotland. The Upper Library, lined with elegant Corinthian columns and lit through the ring of windows in its central dome, is among the finest of the many excellent Neo-classical interiors in Edinburgh.

On the opposite side of the High Street is **Edinburgh City Chambers (22)**, approached through a rather pompous arched screen and a spacious forecourt containing a statue of Alexander the Great taming his horse Bucephalus. The Chambers began life as the Royal Exchange, designed by John Adam and completed in 1761 – one of the first notable buildings of 'classical' Edinburgh, and, with 11 stories at its north end, one of the tallest in the Old Town. As Smollett noted in *The Expedition of Humphry Clinker* (1771), it was not a success with the city's merchants, who preferred to conduct business in the street; so in the early 19th century it was converted for municipal use, and now the city's District Council meets here under the chairmanship of the Lord Provost.

22 *Edinburgh City Chambers, seen here through its heavy rusticated porch, looking towards the northern wing, which contains the Council Chamber.*

From Parliament Square to Abbey Strand

23 *The Tron Kirk's 19th-century steeple is a familiar landmark. The previous one, which Cockburn saw burning down in 1824, was less grand but more picturesque: 'An old Dutch thing . . . there could not be a more beautiful firework'. In this church in 1693 a worshipper was overheard praying 'Lord, have mercy on a' fools and idiots, and particularly on the Magistrates of Edinburgh'. Beyond the Tron the Royal Mile stretches east towards the Canongate, and on the left is the grandiose gable of 199 High Street, a seven-storey tenement of the 18th century.*

Eastward and downhill from the area of St Giles' are several narrow closes whose varied historical associations are sometimes enshrined in their names – for example **Covenant Close**, in which the National Covenant was signed, and **New Assembly Close** which leads to New Assemblies Hall, an attractive Georgian building by Gillespie Graham that has accommodated public dances ('assemblies'), a tavern, a masonic lodge, a bank, the centre for the Royal Scottish Society for the Prevention of Cruelty to Children, and (since 1976) Edinburgh's Wax Museum. Both these closes are to the south, on the right as you descend the High Street; those on the left include **Anchor Close**, where the first editions of *Encyclopaedia Britannica* and of Robert Burns' poems were printed by the printer William Smellie.

At the junction of the High Street and South Bridge stands the **Tron Kirk** (**23**), founded in 1637. It was named after the Tron, a public weighing beam which for long stood close to its door and made the site a popular one for merchants selling their wares (though if they were found to be giving short measure, they were nailed to the beam by their ears). Crowds still foregather in front of the church, to welcome in the New Year. The fine hammerbeam roof is contemporary with the ceiling of Parliament Hill; the grand early-19th-century spire replaces a wooden one which burned down in 1824. The church was closed in 1952, and is to be converted into a tourist centre for the Old Town area.

Crossing the junction of North and South Bridges, the High Street continues

its descent past a further series of tenements and closes, especially thickly clustered on the north side. In the 15th-century **Carrubber's Close** Allan Ramsay had a bookseller's business and later opened a theatre (quickly closed again when the godly city magistrates refused it a licence), and here Sir James Simpson, the discoverer of chloroform, ran a medical dispensary in the 1860s. Above the entrance to **Paisley Close** is a memorial window to the disaster of 1861 when the tenement collapsed, killing 35 inhabitants. One boy was saved from beneath the rubble – shouting, as rescuers dug out the debris, 'Heave awa', lads, ah'm no deid yet' – and his face is carved into the memorial along with a slightly anglicized version of his cry. The incident spurred on the city's programme for restoring and maintaining the Old Town's fabric. **Chalmers Close** gives access to **Holy Trinity Church Hall**, one of the saddest medieval remains in Edinburgh. The original Trinity Church was (to judge from drawings) a most exquisite piece of Gothic architecture, but was demolished in the 19th century to make room for the railway to Waverley. Though the stones were carefully numbered for re-erection on the present site, pilfering depleted the stock so much that only the present Hall could be put together, in 1852, using masonry – some of it still beautiful even as isolated fragments – from the original choir and apse.

Eastward the High Street narrows where a block of buildings projects into the road. Immediately before this 'knuckle' is **Moubray House** (**4**, 1462), one of the oldest houses in Edinburgh, where Daniel Defoe, author of *Robinson Crusoe*, edited a political journal in 1710. Defoe came to Edinburgh in 1706 as an English agent to help negotiate the Act of Union, and for his pains had his windows broken by an anti-Union mob. The 'knuckle' itself is occupied by **John Knox's House** (**24**), which dates from around 1490 but was much added to in the 16th century; its crow-step gable, overhanging wooden galleries, and separate staircases to different levels of the house make it one of the most spectacularly archaic buildings in the Old Town. The great Calvinist preacher probably lived here from 1561 until his death in 1572, and for the past century the house has been maintained as a museum to his memory.

On the south side of this stretch of the street are **South Gray's Close**, which housed Scotland's Royal Mint until 1877; the **Museum of Childhood** in Hyndford's Close, which has an evocative collection of Victorian, Edwardian and later toys, games, and children's books; **Fountain Close**, where in 1574 the printer Thomas Bassendyne issued the first bible to be printed in Scotland; **Tweeddale Court**, containing Tweeddale House (1576, reconstructed by Robert Adam), which has recently become the Scottish Poetry Library; and **World's End Close** – the last close in the High Street before the city gates. The old arched gateway, the Netherbow Port, no longer exists, but its name lives on in the Netherbow Arts Centre of the Church of Scotland, a modern building in the style of the surrounding tenements, which stands next to John Knox's House.

The Netherbow Port used to mark the eastward limit of the city of Edinburgh; the rest of the Royal Mile – the **Canongate** – was a separate burgh, founded by Charter of King David I in 1143, and taking its name from the canons of the Abbey at Holyrood. Being near the Palace of Holyroodhouse and on more level ground, the area developed as the court quarter, and several fine residences were built here. After the court removed to London in the 17th century the Canongate went into decline, but even in the late 18th century it

24 *John Knox's House is a prominent feature of the eastern end of the High Street. The initials 'JM' on its west-facing wall are thought to be those of James Mossman, goldsmith to Mary, Queen of Scots, who was probably responsible for most of the 16th-century additions to the house. The museum inside includes a handsome Oak Room with a painted ceiling of about 1600.*

OVERLEAF
25 *White Horse Close, named after Mary, Queen of Scots' white palfrey, has in turn given its name to a well-known brand of whisky. The stables for Holyroodhouse are thought to have been situated here, before the Inn (1623) became the terminus for coaches to Newcastle and London. During the '45 rebellion the close was the Jacobite headquarters. It was restored in 1964.*

boasted an impressive array of artistocrats among its inhabitants. Many of the old buildings have been well restored in recent years, among them **Chessel's Court** (where the nefarious Deacon Brodie was finally apprehended); the old coaching inn and stables of **White Horse Close (25)**; **Morocco Land**, named after an adventurer of the time of Charles I, Andrew Gray, who retired here after a career of piracy among the Moors; and **Bible Land**, distinguished by the carved shield over its doorway, which bears a text from Psalm 130. Not far from Chessel's Court is **Old Playhouse Close**, where Smollett stayed in 1766 gathering material for *Humphry Clinker*.

Opposite Bible Land stands **Moray House (26)**, one of the finest of all the mansions of the nobility, built in 1628 for Mary Sutton, daughter of Lord Darnley. Charles I visited here on several occasions, and Cromwell used it as a headquarters in 1648. From its overhanging balcony, in 1650, the Marquis of Argyll watched his hated enemy Montrose being led to execution; and in 1707 the Treaty of Union between Scotland and England was signed in a summer-house in the garden (still standing, though now in a mere passageway). In modern times the building has been used as the centre of Moray House College of Education, Scotland's leading teacher-training establishment. A short distance east of Moray House is **Huntly House**, dating from 1570. Its top two storeys, white-plastered timber, overhang the lower two, made of stone — formerly a common feature of Old Town architecture. It is now Edinburgh's chief museum of local history, and among many other exhibits contains a copy of the National Covenant of 1638. Huntly House is often called 'Speaking House', for its front bears several 16th-century plaques replying, in pithy Latin, to criticisms supposedly provoked by the magnificence of the building. When it was restored in 1932, a new plaque was added: *Antiqua tamen Juvenesco* (I'm old, but growing younger).

Opposite Huntly House is the Canongate's **Tolbooth (27)**, the original civic centre of the burgh, a rare survivor of 16th-century municipal architecture (the style is Franco-Scottish). It held Council Rooms and a Courthouse, and was once the gaol of the burgh. Here too is a city museum. **Canongate Church (28)**, just east of the Tolbooth, is a plain cruciform building of 1688; the impressive gabled front is rather spoiled by the rather dwarfish Doric portico forming the entrance. Famous men buried in the churchyard (which contains many interesting monuments) include the economist Adam Smith, who lived almost next door in Panmure Close, and the philosopher Dugald Stewart. Here also is the grave of Robert Fergusson (1750–74), possibly Edinburgh's greatest poet. Overcome by depression at the age of 23, he was tricked into the local madhouse and died there a few months later. Robert Burns, who was much inspired by Fergusson's poetic example ('My elder brother in misfortune / By far my elder brother in the Muse'), paid for the headstone erected here in 1787, inscribed with his own verse tribute to his predecessor. Further east on the south side is **Queensberry House** (1651), home of the 2nd Duke of Queensberry, who was despised for accepting a bribe of over £12,000 to push through the Treaty of Union in 1707.

At the foot of the Canongate the road acquires a northern branch, Abbeyhill. The curious little 16th-century building here is known as **'Queen Mary's Bath House'**, though it was more likely a summer pavilion or even a dovecot. The Royal Mile proper pursues its last few yards along Abbey Strand, which forms the approach to the precincts of **Holyrood Abbey and Palace**.

26 *Moray House — with its distinctive pyramidal gate-piers and, to the right of them, its semi-octagonal stair tower — is named after Margaret, wife of the 4th Earl of Moray. She received it as a gift from her mother, the Dowager Countess of Home, for whom it was built in 1628. In May 1650, when her daughter married Lord Lorne, the guests (including the Marquis of Argyll) watched from the balcony at the left as the Marquis of Montrose was led to execution.*

27 *Canongate Tolbooth, where travellers paid their tolls in order to enter Edinburgh, was built in 1591, though its records go back to 1477. The external staircase gave access to the Council Chamber on the first floor. The prominent projecting clock was added in 1822.*

Holyrood

According to legend King David I, hunting through the wild forest on this spot in 1128, on the Feast of the Exaltation of the Holy Cross, was charged by a stag of enormous size and thrown from his horse. To prevent himself being gored, the King grabbed hold of the stag's antlers and discovered he was holding a crucifix set between the horns. The stag disappeared, leaving the cross in his hands. Directed by a dream that night, he founded an Augustinian abbey of the Holy Rood (Cross) on the site of his miraculous escape. The foundation prospered in medieval times, and at its height the Abbey was a building of great importance and splendour. In the 17th century it was converted to the Chapel Royal and later to the Chapel of the Order of the Thistle; but it suffered severe damage during the 1688 Revolution and began to decay. Badly executed 'restorations' in the 18th century caused the roof to collapse in 1768, and since that time the Abbey has been a splendid ruin; most of what remains is fine 13th-century work (**30**). Its romantic atmosphere inspired Mendelssohn, on a visit in 1829, with the opening movement of his 'Scottish' Symphony. In the Royal Vault beneath are buried several Scottish Kings, including David II (son of Robert the Bruce), James II, James V, and Lord Darnley, 'King-Consort' to Mary, Queen of Scots.

Holyroodhouse is still the official residence of the sovereign in Edinburgh. It began life as the Abbey guest-house, and only in 1501 did James IV start to develop it as a royal palace. The north-west tower, built as the private apartments of his son James V, is all that survives of the Renaissance palace, as the

28 *Canongate Church, seen here from the street, displays its decorative south front, with small pillared portico and side-doors. The cross atop the gable is enclosed in a pair of antlers, a reference to the legend of King David I and the stag.*

building was much damaged by fire in 1543 and further in 1650 after Cromwell had quartered his troops there. Following the Restoration of Charles II the Palace was refashioned around a large arcaded quadrangle much in the style of a contemporary French château; the designer was Sir William Bruce and building was supervised by the King's Master Mason, Robert Mylne. It is an elegant and finely proportioned creation (**31**), in the incomparably dramatic setting of Holyrood Park, overlooked by Arthur's Seat. Bruce's design incorporates a castellated south-west tower that nicely balances James V's north-west one, and joins them with a rusticated screen pierced by the Palace's main entrance.

The oldest part of Holyroodhouse is open to the public, and is entered via the Picture Gallery, where Bonnie Prince Charlie held audiences during the '45 rebellion. The walls are adorned with 111 portraits of Scottish Kings, most of them mythical, beginning with 'Fergus I, B.C. 330' and ending with James VI. Ascribed to a Flemish artist, Jacobus de Wet, they are – in the shrewd opinion of one of the correspondents in *Humphry Clinker* – 'paltry daubings, mostly . . . painted either from the imagination, or porters hired to sit for the purpose'. The Royal Apartments in the north-west tower are principally associated with Mary, Queen of Scots, and are maintained as closely as possible in the style of the period. Here the Catholic Mary was preached to (or rather at) by the militantly Presbyterian John Knox – who published, with Elizabeth I in mind as much as his sovereign Mary, the infamous *First Blast of the Trumpet against the Monstrous Regiment of Women* (1558); and here, at the door of the Audience Chamber, Mary's trusted musician-secretary David Rizzio was murdered before her eyes, on a spot still marked by a brass plaque (and till recent times by a painted bloodstain). The later State Apartments, which include the Throne Room and the Dining Room, decorated in Adam style, are associated with George IV, Victoria, and Albert.

In Palace Yard, before the main entrance, stands a charming ornamental fountain of 1859, designed by Robert Matheson; the various figures adorning it are to designs by Charles Doyle (father of Sir Arthur Conan Doyle), whose reputation as an artist has recently been elevated from obscurity through the publication of a fantastic sketchbook executed in his last years in an Edinburgh asylum.

From Holyrood to Greyfriars Church

Holyrood Road returns to the region of the Old Town, running parallel to and south of the Canongate until it is crossed by the thoroughfare known as the Pleasance. Here we encounter a substantial section of the **Flodden Wall**, which was hastily erected for the defence of the city in the wake of the disastrous Battle of Flodden Field (1513) that destroyed James IV and the flower of Scottish chivalry. The westward path of Holyrood Road is continued by the **Cowgate**, one of Edinburgh's oldest streets and formerly one of the finest. It runs parallel to the High Street but on much lower ground, so the South and George IV Bridges were built across it, reducing it to minor status and canyonlike desolation. It remains the best viewpoint for those bridges, which bear so much of the modern structure of Edinburgh; and it affords access to several interesting buildings, among them the **old Royal High School Building** in Infirmary Street, and the exquisite **St Cecilia's Hall** in Niddry Street. This

30 *The ruined nave and west front of Holyrood Abbey (13th century). The curious tracery network in the west window dates from the 17th century when the nave served as the Chapel of the Order of the Thistle. The Abbey housed a reputed fragment of the True Cross that had belonged to St Margaret; captured in 1346 by the English, this 'Black Rood of Scotland' disappeared at the Reformation.*

31 *The west front of the Palace of Holyroodhouse, seen from Palace Yard. On the left behind the fountain (modelled on a medieval one at Linlithgow palace) is the north-west tower, the only surviving portion of James V's palace.*

latter was built in 1763 for the Edinburgh Musical Society, its construction being subscribed to by no less than 21 earls and many other dignitaries. Its situation was ruined by the South Bridge, which rose towering above it in 1786, but the interior, finely restored in 1966, is beautiful. Modelled on the opera-house at Parma, the Hall is oval, lit by a single chandelier depending from a concave elliptical ceiling. In the late 18th century it was Edinburgh's chief concert-hall, where the most celebrated European musicians performed established masters, such as Handel, and more contemporary music, including works by native composers such as the Earl of Kelly and the violin virtuoso William McGibbon; it also, according to Henry Mackenzie, author of *The Man of Feeling*, 'had the property of shewing off the ladies to great advantage'. Since 1966 the Hall has again been used for concerts, and it houses the Russell Collection of early keyboard instruments for Edinburgh University's Music Department.

Just by St Cecilia's Hall **Blackfriars Street**, formerly Blackfriars Wynd, links the Cowgate and High Street: this was one of the most important streets of the Renaissance town and contained several aristocratic mansions. Their surviving representative is Regent Morton's House, still recognizably a 16th-century construction. The Cowgate continues westward past **Magdalen Chapel**, which should not be judged by its Victorian street front: it was founded in 1541, the interior is good Jacobean work, and it contains the only pre-Reformation Scottish stained glass in its original situation.

Passing under George IV Bridge, the Cowgate enters the **Grassmarket** (**32**), a great rectangular space, formerly the city's cattle market, with a spectacular prospect of the southern cliffs of Castle Rock. At its north-eastern corner are the few remaining buildings of what used to be one of the most picturesque streets

in the city, the old West Bow. Among its inhabitants was the notorious Major Weir, or 'Angelical Thomas', another Scot with a double character (like Brodie); known to his peers as a Covenanting soldier and one of the godliest men of his time, he was burned as a witch in 1670 after he confessed to organizing a coven and committing crimes of the utmost obscenity. His house stood unoccupied for a century, an object of horror and reputed haunting; but like most of West Bow it was swept away in 1829 to be replaced by **Victoria Street**, which is picturesque in its own way. This climbs from the Grassmarket to the street level of George IV Bridge, its arcaded shopfronts surmounted by a pedestrian way – a common solution to the architectural problems of a city largely built on steep slopes (there was another example along Leith Street, until Progress arrived in the shape of the St James' Centre).

On **George IV Bridge's** east side stands the **National Library of Scotland**, properly an extension of the complex of legal buildings in nearby Parliament Square. It is one of the largest libraries in the United Kingdom, founded in 1682 by the Faculty of Advocates, and entitled since 1710 to one copy of every book published in Britain. On the west side of the bridge is **Edinburgh Central Library**, a fine Victorian approximation of Renaissance French style; and at the south end of the bridge a turn to the west leads to the precincts of **Greyfriars Church** (**33**).

The eastern end of this church – the first to be built in Edinburgh after the Reformation – dates from 1620, and its anachronistic Gothic windows and buttresses may have been taken, like its name, from the Franciscan Friary that stood nearby until its dissolution in 1561. In 1722 New Greyfriars, a second church with a similar cross-section, was joined onto the west end, in place of the spire which was destroyed by a gunpowder explosion in 1718. During restoration work in 1938 the dividing wall was removed to create a single long spireless church. The **churchyard** vies with the Old Calton Burial Ground as Edinburgh's most prestigous place of interment, rich in poignant monuments and famous dust (**35**). Some of the memorials are protected with metal lattices to defeat the efforts of body-snatchers (Edinburgh is the city of Burke and Hare). The poet Allan Ramsay, author of *The Gentle Shepherd*, lies here; so do the architects John and Robert Adam; Duncan Forbes of Culloden (see above, p. 32); the philanthropist George Heriot, jeweller to James VI and celebrated in Scott's novel *The Fortunes of Nigel* as 'Jinglin' Geordie'; and James Douglas, Earl of Morton, Regent of Scotland during James VI's minority and executed by him for his part in the murder of James' father Lord Darnley. Here too is an obelisk, inscribed with his own Gaelic verse, to the poet Duncan Ban McIntyre (1724–1812), who was born in Glenorchy and settled in Edinburgh in the 1760s. Unable to read or write, he was a master in the ancient Gaelic oral tradition; his most celebrated poem is the 555-line *Beinn Dorain*, in praise of the Highland mountain of that name – judged by all authorities to be one of the greatest poems in the Gaelic language, which is to say one of the great poems of world literature (there is a modern English translation by Hugh MacDiarmid).

The churchyard is also famous as the first place where the National Covenant was signed, on 28 February 1638; in 1679 over 1,200 Covenanters were imprisoned in a corner of the yard for three months, and many died of exposure and starvation. In delightful contrast to these grim associations is the statue of a little dog by the churchyard gate. **'Greyfriars Bobby'** (**34**) watched over the grave of his master John Gray, a shepherd from the Pentland Hills, for 14 years until his own death in 1872, by which time his loyalty had become so famous that Queen Victoria herself made the suggestion that he should be buried beside his master. His monument is one of the most popular attractions for Edinburgh's visitors.

From Greyfriars to the New Town

Across the road from Greyfriars Bobby, linking George IV Bridge with South Bridge, is Chambers Street, a mid-Victorian thoroughfare running just to the north of Edinburgh University and in itself a kind of academic quarter. On its north side are **Heriot Watt University** (previously a technical college, elevated to university status in 1966) and the **Edinburgh School of Arts**; on the south is the **Royal Scottish Museum**, probably the best general museum in Scotland, with varied and extensive collections imaginatively presented. A perennial attraction for children young and old is the Hall of Power, thronged with intricate working models of transport and machinery from the Industrial Revolution to the present. The Museum's design, by Captain Francis Fowke of the Royal Engineers (architect of London's Royal Albert Hall), is largely in the style of an Italianate palace, but its glory is the vast, bright, airy, and oddly moving entrance hall (**37**), whose tiers of balconies, glazed roof, and soaring, arching, cast-iron pillars and braces are an inspired sublimation of Victorian railway station architecture.

  South Bridge (1785–8), at the eastern end of Chambers Street, was built to provide access to the southerly developments (the 'South Side') which formed the first major expansion of Edinburgh off the east–west axis of the Old Town. The bridge is really an immense viaduct, over 1,000 feet long, flanked on either side by shops and public buildings, so that, except where it spans the Cowgate,

34 *Greyfriars Bobby, the shepherd's faithful friend. Originally his statue had a drinking-fountain for animals attached. On the left is the Guildhall of the Corporation of Candlemakers (1722), which gave Candlemaker Row its name.*

33 *Greyfriars Church: this side view clearly shows its former division into two separate but contiguous buildings.*

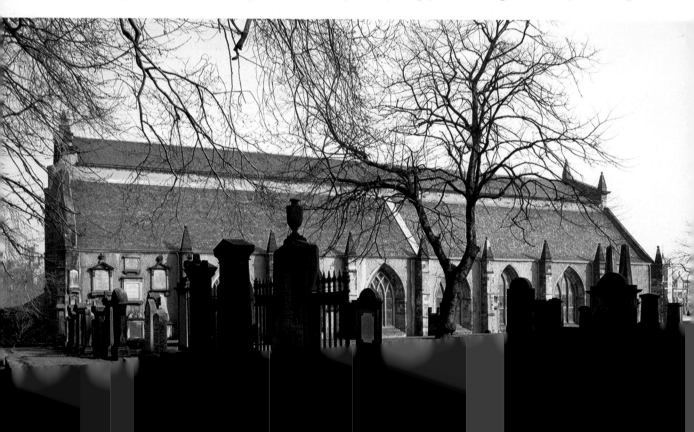

THE
DRINKING WATER
SUPPLY WAS
DISCONTINUED IN
1957

it appears to be just a wide city street. Immediately south of its junction with Chambers Street it passes the entrance of the most notable of all the South Side developments, the **Old College** of the University of Edinburgh (**36**).

Edinburgh's University is the largest in Scotland (though not the oldest, which is St Andrews). Founded in 1582, during the minority of James VI, it initially occupied buildings hastily erected on the site of Kirk o' Field, where a vast explosion had reduced a noble mansion to rubble, killing James' father Lord Darnley. The first intake was of 80 students to study philosophy under Robert Rollock, who had been a professor at St Andrews. Since then the numbers have increased a hundredfold, and the University has developed six main faculties – Arts, Divinity, Law, Medicine, Music, and Science – in all of which it has formed distinguished practitioners, though probably the Medical Faculty is the most famous. In 1983 the Science Faculty established the first-ever chair of parapsychology, under the terms of a bequest by the late Arthur Koestler.

The Old College was erected on the Kirk o' Field site between 1789 and 1834. Its original design was by Robert Adam, and the pillared portico on South Bridge is spoken of as one of his best works; but the College cannot fairly be described as an Adam building, for none of the internal arrangements are his, nor is any elevation as he envisaged it. His plan was elaborate, not to say grandiose, but when he died in 1792 very little had been completed, and construction ceased soon afterwards for lack of funds – which were not to be found again until the end of the Napoleonic Wars. After a competition to bring the design within more modest dimensions while incorporating as many as possible of Adam's ideas, W. H. Playfair was commissioned in 1815 to finish the job. The resulting building is a single large court (rather than Adam's two) with both Grecian and Palladian features. Its finest portion is the **Upper Library**, a structure totally unintended by Adam, 138 feet long, pillared, arched, and

36 *The Quadrangle of the Old College of Edinburgh University, designed by Robert Adam, looking east towards the main entrance – the only substantial portion to be built in Adam's lifetime. The dome was added in the 1880s, and is much larger than he envisaged.*

coffered in white and gold: a magnificent achievement of Edinburgh classicism which stands comparison with the celebrated Wren Library at Trinity College, Cambridge. It is likely that Edinburgh's own near-contemporary Signet Library (see above, p. 32), of which Playfair had designed the main staircase, was his chief inspiration. Also in the west side of the quadrangle is another fine Playfair gallery, the Upper Museum Hall, which housed the Royal Scottish Museum in its early days (before it moved to Chambers Street) and is now the Talbot Rice Arts Centre, combining the Torrie Collection of Renaissance European painting with a gallery for modern art.

On the opposite side of the street from Old College and a little to the south is the grand Ionic portico of **Surgeons' Hall** (1832), another of Playfair's essays in the purest classical style. Clearly he thought of it as a Temple to Medicine; the portico is raised upon a massive wall punctuated by large flanking gates. The impressive museum hall of medical exhibits is worth a visit for those with strong stomachs.

To the south and west of Old College are several important University buildings of more recent date, approached via Teviot Place. The **Reid Concert Hall** of the Faculty of Music is a very respectable essay in Italian Renaissance style for 1858; the name of the Hall and the Music School perpetuates the memory of General John Reid (1721–1807), soldier and composer, who founded the Professorship of Music at the University. (Perhaps the most famous Reid Professor was Donald F. Tovey, whose *Essays in Musical Analysis* were written for the concerts of the Reid Orchestra, which he founded and conducted between the World Wars.) The **McEwan Hall** (completed 1897), used for occasions of University ceremonial, is externally a rather pompous Italianate basilica (**38**) but a powerful, vaulted Byzantine cavern inside; on the circular wall frescoes of enormous figures in pre-Raphaelite style, symbolising the academic virtues, do duty for the expected icons. Further south is the most modern part of the University, constructed in the 1960s round three sides of **George Square** (**9**). This large and once impressive square, built as a private speculation in 1763–4, was the first true square and the first modern residential project in Edinburgh; the demolition of three-quarters of its Georgian housing to make way for the University provoked a public outcry. On the east side now rises the **David Hume Tower** (1963, designed by Robert Matthew). Hume attended the University, though he did not take a degree; it is unlikely that he would have cared much for this 14-storey skyscraper block, though it commands excellent views of Arthur's Seat and Salisbury Crags, and was the first modern building to make a serious contribution to the Edinburgh skyline. Also on this side of the square is the **Appleton Tower** (1966) of science laboratories and lecture theatres; and along the south side is the elegant rectangular sweep of the eight-storey **University Library** (1967), by Sir Basil Spence – one of the city's more attractive modern buildings. Its important collections of books include the library of William Drummond of Hawthornden (1585–1649), the poet sometimes called 'the Scottish Petrarch'. Lauriston Place leads away from this area past the **University Medical School**, completed in 1888 in Venetian Renaissance style. Famous physicians who have lectured in the Medical School include the anaesthetist James Young Simpson and the surgeon Joseph Lister. Its best-remembered student, however, is probably Sir Arthur Conan Doyle, who found inspiration for the character of Sherlock Holmes in Dr Joseph Bell, a surgeon at the neighbouring Royal Infirmary renowned for his powers of

37 *London's long-vanished Crystal Palace may have been the inspiration for the Entrance Hall of the Royal Scottish Museum, one of the most elegant examples of the structural use of cast iron to survive from the Victorian era.*

observation and deductive reasoning. The **Royal Infirmary** can be seen on the south side of Lauriston Place, flaunting the pointed turrets of romantic Franco-Scottish castle architecture. Begun in 1870, its design was influenced by practical advice from Florence Nightingale.

To the north of Lauriston Place, set in its own grounds, is **George Heriot's Hospital School** (**39**), possibly the most opulent Renaissance building in Scotland. The munificent 'Jinglin' Geordie' endowed it from the bulk of his estate as a school for the teaching of 'puir fatherless bairns', and it eventually opened in 1659 with 30 pupils, although the building had already been used as a hospital by Cromwell during the Civil War. Since then it has been one of Edinburgh's leading schools, and in its way it provides as splendid an architectural environment as the severely classical Royal High School (see below, p. 70). With its pinnacled towers and turrets it could easily be mistaken for a palace. There are 200 windows, no two alike: the most elaborate look into the inner courtyard, where many are enriched with tracery (some being set in pointed arches), and others are surmounted by intricately carved decoration.

Leading north off Lauriston Place, west of George Heriot's, is the **Vennel**, a narrow passage like a long wynd, which descends by steps back to the Grassmarket. Along the eastern side of these steps runs another portion of the Flodden Wall, the best still standing, including the remains of one of the defensive towers that originally punctuated it.

The Grassmarket terminates at its western end with the West Port, through which Bonnie Prince Charlie's army entered Edinburgh during the '45 rebellion. In this area the 'resurrection men' Burke and Hare were most active,

38 The imposing exterior of the McEwan Hall, designed for the University in 1875 by Sir R. Rowand Anderson and completed in 1897.

39 *George Heriot's Hospital School, erected 1628–59, used to be attributed to Inigo Jones, but it is more likely to be the work of the master masons William Wallace and William Ayton, in collaboration with the then Dean of Rochester, who was nephew and executor of the benefactor George Heriot.*

murdering indigents and drunks for the dissecting table of the renowned anatomist Robert Knox, who was brought to trial in 1828. The other way out of the Old Town on this side is King's Stables Road, which swings round the lee of the Castle to bring the traveller onto Lothian Road and to **St Cuthbert's Church and Churchyard** (**40**), set below the road level in what is now the extreme western end of Princes Street Gardens. This is the oldest church site in Edinburgh, dating back – like St Margaret's Chapel – to the reign of Malcolm III. However, the present building, apart from its 18th-century steeple, dates from the 1890s and was designed in Renaissance style by Hippolyte Blanc. It is worth visiting for its serene churchyard, burial place of Thomas de Quincey, the author of *Confessions of an English Opium Eater*, and of the mathematician John Napier of Merchiston, who in 1614 established the theoretical basis of logarithms. Immediately north of St Cuthbert's, and raised above it to the level of the junction of Lothian Road and Princes Street, is the diminutive **St John's Church** by William Burn, which John Ruskin admired – an imaginative piece of Gothic revival with unexpectedly impressive fan-vaulting in the nave, the pendants suggesting the influence of St George's Chapel, Windsor.

Both these churches belong properly to the area and history of the New Town, but both (as mentioned at the beginning of this chapter) are excellent viewpoints for the western crags of Castle Rock. The visitor surveying the Castle across the open expanse of Princes Street Gardens may find it hard to imagine this area submerged beneath the stagnant waters of the Nor' Loch, as it was until the mid-18th century. The disappearance of that barrier to northward expansion marked the emergence of a new Edinburgh.

3 The New Towns

The New Town of Edinburgh, one of the boldest schemes of civic architecture in the history of Europe, was essentially the brain-child of the forceful and imaginative George Drummond (1687–1766), five times Lord Provost of the city between 1725 and 1764. Through his efforts Government permission was obtained to extend the city northwards onto a rectangular plateau known as Barefoot's Parks, on the far side of the Nor' Loch. Access was to be by the North Bridge, on which construction began in 1765. The following year a competition was announced for the 'Plans of a New Town marking out streets of a proper breadth, and by-lanes, and the best situation for a reservoir, and any other public buildings, which may be thought necessary . . .'. The winner was an unknown 22-year-old architect, James Craig, and over the next half-century his plan was almost precisely adhered to.

Craig achieved brief celebrity through his success in the competition but died in debt and obscurity in 1795. A nephew of James Thomson (the poet of *The Seasons*), he seems to have been a man of modest gifts. Hardly any examples of his buildings survive, and the New Town plan, although its large-scale unity was unprecedented in British urban architecture, has been criticized as painfully regular (it is all squares and rectangles) and old-fashioned in the European context. But its cardinal virtue is the thoroughgoing use made of the available space. Single-sided terraces – Princes Street and Queen Street – face respectively south (to the Castle and High Street) and north (towards the Firth of Forth). Between them, the plateau's high spine, previously known as the Lang Dykes, carries a grand central thoroughfare, George Street, linking two great civic squares: St Andrew in the east and St George's (later Charlotte Square) in the west. In its naïve fashion the design symbolized the union of Scotland and England, conjoined in the person of the King; and two long lanes, either side of George Street and parallel to it, extended the symbolism by referring to the national emblems in their names, Thistle Street and Rose Street. Stiff and geometrical the plan may be, but on the ground it has all the grandeur that simplicity can bestow.

Craig was not responsible for, and perhaps did not foresee, the excellence of the buildings that were constructed – to the very general specifications laid down by the town Council – along his spacious rectilinear grid. One of the fearfully symmetrical details in his conception was that two imposing churches, St Andrew's and St George's, should face each other along George Street from the far sides of their respective squares. But within a month of permission being given, in 1767, to build on the New Town area, the wealthy Sir Laurence

40 *St Cuthbert's Church and its peaceful churchyard, where the Old and New Towns meet.*

Dundas had contrived to obtain the site intended for St Andrew's Church, on which he proceeded to build himself a magnificent town house to a design by Sir William Chambers. In the 19th century the building became the headquarters of the **Royal Bank of Scotland**, and was enlarged to include a light, airy, Pantheon-like circular Telling Room with a star-spangled cupola reminiscent of the tomb of the Empress Galla Placidia in Ravenna (**41**).

The Royal Bank was only one of many banks, insurance businesses, and legal firms to occupy premises in **St Andrew Square**, which began life as a fashionable residential area, and has been called one of the wealthiest squares in the world. Many of the buildings constructed in the first century of its existence are in a monumental Graeco-Roman style (such as No. 38, now the Bank of Scotland) or modelled on Renaissance palazzos (**43**). The slab-like sides of the modern office development in St David's Street do not exactly harmonize with the whole, but answer to their surroundings in monumentality. The central gardens of the Square are dominated by the massive 100-foot pillar carrying a statue of the lawyer and statesman Henry Dundas, first Viscount Melville (1742–1811), chief ally of William Pitt the Younger and one of the most powerful men of his time – Cockburn described him in 1800 as 'absolute dictator of Scotland'.

Cheated of its intended situation by the crafty Sir Laurence, **St Andrew's Church** was eventually completed in 1785 in George Street itself. The Council acquired its site from the original lease-holder (*feuar* in Scots legal terminology), one John Young, who was compensated with land immediately adjacent to it and was able to impose various conditions, among them that there should be no burials on the church ground. St Andrew's is accordingly a church without a churchyard, and was soon hemmed in by surrounding buildings (**42**). The tall, thin spire, added in 1789, rather over-balances the design of the exterior, which is clearly based on the Pantheon, with a Corinthian portico leading into an auditorium. However the auditorium is not circular like the Pantheon but a delicate oval, and this configuration, possibly a conscious echo of St Cecilia's Hall, shapes a most beautiful classical interior, with some exquisite plasterwork decoration on the flat ceiling (**44**).

Many of the other notable buildings in George Street are temples of a different kind, 'Temples to Mammon'. The monumental banks and insurance houses dotted along it sport some of the finest examples of 19th-century classical and Renaissance façades to be found in any single street in Britain, in a slightly dizzying profusion of porticos, pediments, and pilasters. Among the more restrained of them is 45 George Street, now a French bank, originally the offices of William Blackwood the publisher and of his famous *Blackwood's Magazine*. The **Assembly Rooms and Music Hall**, built by public subscription in 1784–7, with a classical portico added 1818, is now a conference centre. It retains a sumptuous Adam-style ballroom, and is still used for concerts and other functions during the Festival, as is the **Freemasons' Hall** (1912), further along to the west, with its ornate clerestoried interior.

Hanover Street, Frederick Street, and Castle Street, which traverse George Street and divide it into four equal segments, are on the whole less interesting, though there are good shopping areas in their south arms. But **North Castle Street** is worth looking at for its pleasing flats built in 1793, where Sir Walter Scott lived (at No. 39) from 1802 to 1826 and wrote most of the Waverley novels. At each of the three crossings stands a statue (**45**): George IV; William

41 *The sumptuous interior of the Royal Bank of Scotland in St Andrew Square; this Telling Room, whose iron dome is pierced by glazed coffers in the shape of six-pointed stars, was added to the original mansion in 1857.*

Pitt the Younger; and Dr Chalmers, leader of the Disruption of the Church of Scotland, which took place in St Andrew's Church in 1843. His is the most westerly of the three; continuing in this direction George Street emerges into its other great terminus **Charlotte Square** (46).

Whereas St Andrew Square developed into an architecturally various commercial centre, Charlotte Square has remained primarily residential and homogenous. Designed by Robert Adam in 1791 (the last year of his life), it is widely held to be his masterpiece, and is certainly one of the loveliest large residential squares in Europe. Each side is designed as an integral unit, and the houses are on a grand scale, uniformly three storeys high with attic and basement. Yet such is the square's width (500 feet) that the richly and gracefully decorated façades do not oppress; and the equestrian statue of Prince Albert in the spacious central garden – famous for its crocuses in early spring – is no inescapable public proclamation like the Melville Column in St Andrew Square. The north side is the oldest portion, and the best preserved. But it is the total effect that gives greatest pleasure: a quarter of a million square feet summing up all that is best in Edinburgh classicism.

Charlotte Square was for long known as 'Edinburgh's Harley Street' because of the number of doctors who settled there, Joseph Lister among them. Earl Haig, British commander in France during World War I, was born at No. 24. No. 19 is now the headquarters of the Scottish Arts Council, and No. 6 is the official residence of the Secretary of State for Scotland (47). The National Trust for Scotland has its offices in No. 5, and administers the lower floors of No. 7 as a showpiece 'Georgian House', open to the public; the upper floors are the official residence of the Moderator of the General Assembly of the Church of Scotland. On the western side, looking down George Street, is **St George's Church** – if anything the weakest building in the square. Adam had designed a finer one than this, but after his death his scheme was dropped on grounds of cost, and St George's was erected in 1811–14 to a design by Robert Reid. The front is rather dull, with over-large Ionic columns in a recessed portico, but the tall green copper dome, a creative echo of St Paul's Cathedral in London, makes handsome amends. The building is no longer a church, having been converted to serve as West Register House in the 1960s: it is open to the public, and historical documents are on display.

From Charlotte Square, Charlotte Street leads north and slightly downhill to connect with **Queen Street**, the northern terrace of James Craig's New Town plan. Its pleasant situation (away from the traffic of Princes Street and the Old Town, looking instead over the gardens to what was then open country and the Firth of Forth) made it a prime residential area from the New Town's earliest years. The painter Henry Raeburn had his studio in York Place, at the eastern end; Sir James Simpson lived at No. 52, and discovered the properties of chloroform there; and Chopin gave one of his last recitals in 1848 at the Hopetoun Rooms, No. 72. No. 9, the splendidly imitation-Roman **Royal College of Physicians**, is – inside and out – one of the most inventive designs of Thomas Hamilton (1784–1858), another talented Edinburgh architect, whose masterpiece we shall encounter in the Royal High School. Apart from this, the street's chief feature is a huge late-19th-century building immediately north of St Andrew Square housing the **Scottish National Portrait Gallery and National Museum of Antiquities**, which proves that red sandstone is not appropriate material for a version of the Doge's Palace. The museum contains

42 *This view of the eastern end of George Street shows how the delicate St Andrew's Church (centre) has been hemmed in by grander, less spiritual structures. The building to the left is one of the city's oldest-established hotels, The George, and is typical of the Graeco-Roman style of architecture that characterises the street.*

several fine collections, among them the Roman treasure excavated from Traprain Law near Melrose (associated by Rosemary Sutcliffe in her popular children's novel *The Eagle of the Ninth* with the destruction of the Ninth Legion in the early 2nd century), an interesting range of medieval and Renaissance armour, and Edinburgh's much-used guillotine, 'The Maiden'. The Portrait Gallery, which was initially funded by the private fortune of J. R. Findlay, editor of *The Scotsman*, contains a wide-ranging selection of portraits of famous Scots from the 16th century to the present. Among its latest acquisitions are a portrait of an Edinburgh doctor by the celebrated 19th-century mad artist Richard Dadd, and a specially commissioned portrait by Victoria Crowe of the composer-pianist Ronald Stevenson.

The Eastern New Town and Calton Hill

The visitor emerges from the eastern end of Queen Street in York Place, to be confronted by the sudden fantastic prospect of the **Calton Hill**: another of Edinburgh's dead volcanoes, surmounted by an acropolis of picturesque structures. It is only since the shops and tenements that lined Leith Street were demolished in the early 1970s that this spectacular view has become available, and it may not last much longer; the near slope of the grassy bank that now separates the road from the hill, cropped in the hours before dawn by a vigorous population of rabbits, is earmarked for BBC Scotland's new Broadcasting Centre. Calton Hill and its environs form the nucleus of the so-called Eastern New Town, in which the ideas and ideals of the late 18th century were re-thought by the next generation, and they reward exploration.

It is possible to take a clockwise route almost right round the Hill by following **Royal Terrace**, **Carlton Terrace**, and **Regent Terrace**, which leads via Regent Road and Waterloo Place back westwards to the junction of Princes Street and Leith Street. These terraces originated in a series of proposals for an Eastern New Town (envisaged as extending to the port of Leith) by the Glasgow architect William Stark. Unlike James Craig and his contemporaries, Stark had a startlingly modern approach to the issues of town layout. Deploring symmetry and uniformity as empty conceits, he recommended making the utmost use of existing natural features, from standing trees to the broad sweep of scenery and landscape. When he submitted these proposals he was already seriously ill, and he died soon afterwards, in 1813, still a young man. Scott thought him a genius; Cockburn said he was 'the best modern architect Scotland had produced'. After another competition W. H. Playfair, who had briefly studied with Stark, was entrusted with realising his vision, and designed the terraces around Calton Hill. At their least appealing, as in the grim and colonnaded Royal Terrace, the buildings have a grand sobriety; at their best, in Regent Terrace, they form what has often justly been declared the most

44 *The atmospheric interior of St Andrew's Church. Like many of the New Town buildings, the church was the winning design in a competition: the ten-guinea prize went to a plan by a Major Andrew Fraser, which was executed by the architect David Kay.*

45 *The statues of George Street: King George IV, the statesman William Pitt the Younger, and Thomas Chalmers D.D. The king's statue commemorates his state visit in 1824. Dr Chalmers led a faction which demanded the abolition of lay patronage in the Church of Scotland, and which eventually seceded to form the Free Church, without property or endowments. This 'Disruption' broke the State Church's monopoly on education and the administration of relief for the poor.*

beautiful of all Regency streets, not excepting those in Bath. The site could not be bettered: Royal Terrace is offset and humanized by the long wooded gardens on the slope below it, and Regent Terrace is ennobled by its dramatic vista of Arthur's Seat and Salisbury Crags, seen over the deep valley that contains Holyrood and the Canongate.

At the western end of Regent Terrace, where it joins Regent Road, is the **Monument to Robert Burns** (1830), in the inappropriate style of a small circular Greek temple (**49**). But here too, set back into the southern cliffs of the Calton Hill, is one of the finest, and certainly the most extensive, of Edinburgh's Greek temple complexes, the **Royal High School** building (**50**), constructed 1825–9 to a design by Thomas Hamilton, architect of the Burns Monument and a former pupil of the School. The 'Royal High' is the oldest school in Scotland, dating back to the foundation of Holyrood Abbey in 1128. Its pupils have included Robert Adam, George Borrow, Alexander Graham Bell, James Boswell, Lord Chancellor Brougham, Lord Cockburn, Lord Provost Drummond, the poet William Drummond of Hawthornden, King Edward VII (for a term), Robert Fergusson, Francis Jeffrey (noted judge as well as founder and editor of the *Edinburgh Review*), the novelist Henry Mackenzie, and Sir Walter Scott – and more recently the actor Ian Charleson, star of *Chariots of Fire*. The school's building on Regent Road was erected because of severe overcrowding in its previous premises near the Cowgate; in 1970, for the same reason, it migrated to a grossly inferior modern pile at Barnton on the western outskirts of

46 *Charlotte Square: this view, from its south-east corner, looks across the central gardens to West Register House, formerly St George's Church, and gives some idea of the square's great extent.*

47 *No. 6 Charlotte Square – with characteristic New Town street-lamps – in the centre of the square's north side, is the official residence of the Secretary of State for Scotland.*

48 *Herralds Antique Furniture Store in Queen Street, an example of the fine shop frontages to be found throughout the New Town. Note how the stepped design makes light of the street's pronounced slope.*

the city, and the Regent Road building has since been reserved as the home of a hypothetical Scottish Assembly, which awaits devolution to come into being.

Arx in colle sita, 'a citadel sited on a hill', as the school song proclaimed, the complex has been variously described as a copy of the Hephaisteion at Athens or of the Temple of Diana at Ephesus. It is a monumental achievement of Edinburgh classicism, with an exceptionally impressive Doric central block sporting a massive pillared portico and side-galleries. Within this central temple building, when it was still a school, was the remarkable assembly hall, shaped as an oval amphitheatre with a surrounding balcony carried by elegant cast-iron columns, the whole covered by a shallow coffered ceiling. Few schools have ever had a focus of such atmospheric magnificence: a little of this can still be sensed, but the memorial windows and ceremonial exit door have disappeared to Barnton, and the recent modifications to the hall as a parliamentary Debating Chamber – used only occasionally by the Scottish Sub-committee of Westminster MPs – have been wholly insensitive.

Regent Road continues west past **St Andrew's House** (on the south side), the administrative headquarters of the Secretary of State for Scotland, a huge brooding slab-sided construction of the 1930s which has been compared (not inaptly) to an Art Deco mantelpiece clock. Beside it stands **Governor's House**, the only surviving portion of the Old Calton Goal, and another of Edinburgh's thronged cemeteries, the **Calton Old Burial Ground**. Here are Robert Adam's memorial to David Hume, said to be modelled on the tomb of Theodoric in

Ravenna (**53**); Thomas Hamilton's monument to the political martyrs of 1794; the graves of William Blackwood, founder of *Blackwood's Magazine*, and Archibald Constable, Sir Walter Scott's publisher; and a memorial to the Scottish-American soldiers who fought in the American Civil War, erected by George Bissett of New York in 1893 and surmounted by a statue of Abraham Lincoln.

Quite apart from its architectural excitements and historic associations (see below), the top of Calton Hill (355 feet) must be visited for the breathtaking panorama it commands of the whole of central Edinburgh, the Pentland Hills, the Firth of Forth, and the Forth Bridges. The view remains splendid even since the erection to the west of the St James' Centre (1970), a vast grey shopping and hotel complex of undeniable convenience and quite remarkable hideousness, like a prefabricated concrete lavatory built for a race of giants. To make way for this it was necessary to pull down the severe but decently Neoclassical St James' Square, which had been allowed to become derelict – one of the few groups of buildings actually known to have been designed by James Craig. Now Craig's very last identified building overlooks the scene: the **Old Observatory** (1776), perched on the west brow of the Calton Hill. Astonishingly, for the framer of the severe New Town Plan, it is a fantasy Gothic castle, clinging to the lava rocks, wholly improbable and impractical, with a fairy-tale charm. It now forms one corner of the much larger **New Observatory**, built by Playfair in 1818 at the greatest possible stylistic remove: this is another ultra-civilized classical temple, on a cruciform ground-plan with the domed telescope room in the centre. The architect's uncle John Playfair, a well-known mathematician and natural philosopher, was one of the prime movers in the establishment of a city observatory, so it is fitting that he should be commemorated by the **Playfair Monument**, a large serenely classical cenotaph which his nephew placed at the south-eastern corner of the surrounding wall.

The Calton is a hill of monuments (**52**). Just south-west of the observatory, near a 17th-century cannon that points straight down Princes Street, is the **Monument to Dugald Stewart**, the philosopher. An adherent of David Hume, Stewart (1753–1828) was a professor at the University, lecturing on mathematics, astronomy, and moral philosophy; his most celebrated work is his *Philosophy of the Human Mind*. His momument is another Playfair design, in the shape of a small circular temple (like Hamilton's Burns Monument, but better). A little further south, overlooking Regent Road, is **Nelson's Monument**, a battlemented Gothic tower built in the shape of 108-foot stone telescope standing on its broad end. It was designed soon after the Battle of Trafalgar but only completed in 1816. A stump mast with crosstrees at the top of the tower flies Nelson's famous 'England expects . . .' signal every Trafalgar Day; and every weekday, synchronizing with the Castle's One-o'-clock gun, a large ball descends from the mast to mark the time for those out of earshot, especially the ships in the Firth of Forth.

All these are remarkable enough. But the most bizarre structure on the Calton Hill, standing just east of the Observatory, is a gaunt skeletal portico of twelve huge pillars, a portico into nothing but the ambient air. This is all that remains of an over-ambitious scheme for a **National Monument** dedicated to the memory of those who fell in the Napoleonic Wars, launched by a public subscription appeal in 1822. The intention was to construct 'a facsimile of the Parthenon', incorporating catacombs for the burial of Scotland's greatest men –

49 *'I am a bard of no regard / Wi' gentle folk an' a' that', wrote Robert Burns in* The Jolly Beggars; *30 years after his death he merited Thomas Hamilton's monument to him, a circular Greek temple with Corinthian peristyle.*

national temple and mausoleum in one. C. R. Cockerell, the leading contemporary classical architect, did the preliminary designs, which Playfair, appointed his co-architect, freely adapted while supervising the construction: but the money ran out in 1829 with only the portico, less than five per cent of the whole, in place. To judge by the existing drawings, the completed monument would have been of preposterous size, dwarfing the hill it stood upon, so perhaps the inglorious outcome was for the best. The pillars of 'Edinburgh's Disgrace', as the fragment came to be called, can seem to have a romantic, rather crazy beauty, making the Calton's grassy summit a dream landscape devised for a painting by Claude Lorrain.

From Regent Road the area of the original New Town can be regained by way of **Waterloo Place**, built in 1815 as the first road link to the new eastern developments. For much of its length the 'Place' is another of Edinburgh's incognito bridges, only revealing its true nature in the span called Regent Bridge, a high wide arch carrying the roadway over the Calton Road. Regent Bridge also bears a Napoleonic War memorial in the shape of a Corinthian arch.

Along Princes Street

Waterloo Place leads past Leith Street straight into the eastern end of **Princes Street**, the southern terrace of Craig's plan, Edinburgh's centre, the city's main shopping street, and one of the most scenically spectacular streets in the world. Along a stretch of over three-quarters of a mile New Town confronts Old Town across the valley now occupied by Princes Street Gardens, and here many state processions and parades take place; every weekday of the Festival there is a parade of pipers from different Scottish regiments and institutions.

50 *Thomas Hamilton's Royal High School building (1825–9), once described by Sir John Summerson as 'the noblest monument of the Scottish Greek Revival'. It is now an art gallery.*

51 *Arthur's Seat from Calton Hill. The nearest portion is the massive Salisbury Crags, with the diminutive path of the Radical Road winding at its foot.*

Immediately on the left as one enters Princes Street from the east is the grim and grandiose Victorian **General Post Office**, on a site once occupied by Edinburgh's Old Theatre Royal and the tiny Shakespeare Square, one of the first developments in the new Town area. Its Philatelic Bureau has a gallery for the display of interesting postage stamps. On the right is an even earlier and fortunately still standing development: the sumptuous **Register House** (1774–1834), one of the most celebrated buildings of Robert Adam. Grand in scale but beautifully proportioned, it has an impressive entrance stairway and Corinthian portico with a dome behind over the central hall, and square pavilions at all four corners, each carrying a diminutive and graceful clock tower. The building is the headquarters of the Scottish Record Office and houses Scottish historical and legal documents – including birth, marriage, and death certificates, wills, and census records – dating as far back as the 13th century (some of the more modern holdings are stored in West Register House in Charlotte Square). Immediately behind is **New Register House**, a 19th-century extension that contains the offices of the Registrar-General for Scotland and Scotland's chief authority on heraldry, the Lord Lyon King of Arms.

Standing before the entrance to Register House is a splendid equestrian statue, by Sir John Steell, of the Duke of Wellington (**54**): 'The Iron Duke in bronze by Steell', as the contemporary quip had it when the figure was installed in 1852. (There are several more of Steell's statues in the Princes Street area.) Although Wellington is appropriately visible, in profile, from Waterloo Place,

his outstretched arm points straight up **North Bridge**, which joins Princes Street from the south opposite Register House. Originally built in the 1760s as the main artery between Old and New Towns, the bridge was completely rebuilt in the 1890s and now spans the valley above the roofs of Waverley Station. Unlike its southern continuation, South Bridge, there is no disguising the fact that it is a gigantic 'fly-over', and the effect of its junction with the Old Town, slicing into the tall buildings between the offices of the *Scotsman* newspaper and the Calton Hotel, is highly dramatic. It enters the New Town between the G.P.O. and the North British Railway Hotel; westward past the hotel and beyond the Waverley Steps which lead down into the station the true glory of Princes Street comes into full view – its south side, unbuilt on except for some memorials, with its outlook towards the Old Town and the Castle, over **Princes Street Gardens**.

The Gardens, formed by draining the Nor' Loch in the 1760s, were not part of Craig's plan: he seems to have envisaged a kind of ornamental canal here. There were some bitter legal battles in the early 19th century to prevent eager speculators from constructing houses and shops along the south side, but from the 1820s the area has been purposely preserved. Landscaped and criss-crossed with tree-lined avenues, it is perhaps the most attractive, as well as the most central, of the Edinburgh public parks. The railway line to Glasgow was driven right through it in 1847, but (especially in the western half) is nestled discreetly in a cutting below the level of the valley bottom: its stone wall, tunnels, and embankment are by the ubiquitous Playfair.

52 *Looking west on the summit of Calton Hill: Nelson's Monument (left) and the portico of the unfinished National Monument (right) frame the distant shapes of the observatory complex, including James Craig's Old Observatory (centre left) and the Playfair Monument (centre right).*

In Eastern Princes Street Gardens, just by the roadway, towers the **Walter Scott Monument** (1844), a fantastically ornate piece of Gothic masonry that may suggest comparison with the later Albert Memorial in London, but is on a far vaster scale, over 200 feet high (**1, 21, 55**). It was the winning design in an open competition, and is the work of George Meikle Kemp, a self-taught architect, son of a shepherd. Kemp was drowned while the monument was still under construction, and it remains his only building of any importance; the sky-piercing energy of the spire testifies to an original and vigorous talent. Beneath the arched canopy of the supporting pillars is a seated statue of Scott by Sir John Steell, and in 64 separate niches are statuettes of characters from Scott's novels. The monument is open to the public: a 287-step staircase ascends to a platform near the top of the spire that offers wonderful views (especially the vertiginous one straight down into Princes Street).

A little further to the west Princes Street Gardens are divided in two by the **Mound**, a great artificial slope that carries a roadway from George IV Bridge in the Old Town down to Princes Street and the south end of Hanover Street in the New Town. This was formed by depositing the earth excavated in the building of the New Town, and was at first called simply 'the earthen mound'. At its north end now stand two of Edinburgh's most notable classical buildings, housing two of her most important artistic institutions: the **Royal Scottish Academy** and the **National Gallery of Scotland** (**58**). Both are by Playfair, and both are in the Greek revival style so beloved of New Town architects. The older (the more northerly, fronting onto Princes Street) is the Academy, built in the 1820s but enlarged and much improved in the following decade: a long low

53 *Old Calton Burial Ground: the cylindrical David Hume memorial by Robert Adam. The headstone to the left of it with the medallion commemorates the history painter David Allan (1744–96).*

Doric temple, complete with sphinxes, much decorative carving, and a massive but engaging statue of the young Queen Victoria (by Steell) on the roof. The R.S.A., established in 1826 to encourage the fine arts in Scotland, has presented an annual exhibition of painting and sculpture by its members every year since 1827, and mounts special exhibitions during the Festival. Immediately behind the Academy, the National Gallery, designed by Playfair in 1845 and opened in 1859, is a striking contrast to the robustness of the earlier building – an Ionic temple this time, with its principal porticos on the long side. The long window-less walls, rhythmically enlivened by shallow pilasters, are elegant as well as monumental. The collection is a distinguished one: there is naturally a section devoted to Scottish artists, but the majority of the paintings and sculptures are English and European works from the 14th century to the present day. The finest of the individual exhibits, which include such masterpieces as G.B. Tiepolo's *The Finding of Moses* and Poussin's *Sacraments*, are mostly on permanent loan from the collection of the Duke of Sutherland.

Between these galleries and East Princes Street Gardens is a wide space customarily used as Edinburgh's 'Speakers' Corner', and on the other side of the Mound lies **West Princes Street Gardens**, beautifully sited under the looming crags of the Castle. This section contains several prominent monuments, within the gardens but level with the street, including one to Sir James Galton Simpson; one to the philanthropic minister Dr Guthrie; Steell's statue of Allan Ramsay; and the equestrian monument (horse and rider a third larger than life-size) to the members of Scotland's crack cavalry regiment, the Scots Greys, who fell in South Africa during the Boer War. Also in these Gardens is a memorial to Scots Americans killed in the Great War (**56**), and the modern (1942) Royal Scots Monument to the regiment of that name, at the western slope of the Mound. Near to the Allan Ramsay statue, the celebrated **Floral Clock** – built in 1903, and the oldest of its kind in the world – tells the time in summer with face, hands, and numerals laid out in 24,000 brightly coloured flowers and foliage plants. Further west in the valley-bottom lies the Ross Bandstand, scene of many concerts by military and other bands throughout the summer months. Behind the bandstand a footbridge crosses the sunken railway line, and a path by the base of the Castle Rock leads to the ruined and secluded **Wellhouse Tower**, one of the oldest buildings in the city, dating from the reign of King David II (1329–71).

On its north side, Princes Street is a great shopping thoroughfare (the Oxford Street of Edinburgh) and a cheerful architectural jumble. There are still some large and elegant 19th-century commercial buildings, typically combining a department store in the lower half with a hotel above: **Jenners**, an ornate 1890s store somewhat reminiscent of Harrods in London, is the best surviving example. But much Victorian work has been demolished in recent decades and replaced by modern developments. In the 1960s a 'Princes Street Panel' was established in the hope of creating a 20th-century homogeneity for the street-fronts in the spirit of the Georgian unity of the New Town's original architects; it did not survive, but its intentions can be seen in the present British Home Stores building and the angular blue-granite New Club (1966), which replaced a 19th-century club building. Uniformity in Princes Street is a lost cause, but hardly seems worth striving for: the grandeur of its outlook compensates for all architectural irregularities.

Rose Street, the lane running parallel to Princes Street on its north side,

54 *The Duke of Wellington statue at the east end of Princes Street, silhouetted against the sky and framed by the North British Hotel (left) and Woolworth's store (right).*

should not be overlooked. Until recent times this was a disreputable district, known as Edinburgh's 'Amber Mile' on account of its multitudinous pubs – and for that reason a favoured haunt of Edinburgh's literati, heroic boozers to a man, and a centre of the 'Scottish Literary Renaissance' of the 1930s. The poets Hugh MacDiarmid (C.M. Grieve), Sidney Goodsir Smith, and Robert Garioch, the great Gaelic poet Sorley Maclean, the novelist Eric Linklater, and the essayist and broadcaster Hector McIver have all haunted it. MacDiarmid, Scotland's national poet of the 20th century, was the moving spirit of the Renaissance, re-emphasizing dialect and the achievement of medieval Scots poets like William Dunbar. He found many lesser imitators ('Men of sorrow and acquainted with Grieve' – Edwin Muir), and these especially could be found staked out in the Rose Street pubs. But since the early 1970s Rose Street has become an 'alternative' shopping street and picturesque pedestrian precinct, almost entirely 'dry'. Edinburgh's most famous modern literary pub still stands, however, not in Rose Street but in West Register Street by Register House – the **Café Royal**, its interior a feast of late Victorian ceramic murals, stained glass, and plasterwork.

At the West End of Princes Street stands St John's Episcopal Church (see above, p. 55), and several roads fan out in different directions. Lothian Road leads south by St John's and St Cuthbert's churches in the direction of the domed octagonal **Usher Hall** (Edinburgh's chief concert hall, where the Scottish National Orchestra plays every week during the concert season) and the King's Theatre, the cramped venue still used for opera performances during the Festival. On Lothian Road's west side, opposite St John's, stands the huge **Caledonian Hotel** ('The Caley' in Edinburgh parlance), an opulent be-columned and be-gabled nonsense of the 1890s, built directly on top of the now disused Caledonian Station, at one time a busy terminus for trains from the west. The hotel's plan is almost V-shaped, with the point towards Princes Street; along the south-westerly arm of the V is Rutland Street, leading to **Rutland Square**, the only square in the New Town south of Princes Street, and the smallest; an elegant if rather narrow development of 1819–40.

The Western New Town

The most direct continuation of Princes Street leads into the area of the Western New Town. Throughout the 19th century Edinburgh continued to expand outwards in a great semicircle from Craig's development on the plateau, east, west, and north into the surrounding countryside until it reached the Firth of Forth. Each of these directions has its own 'New Town' marking the beginning of that progress. We have already seen something of the Eastern New Town centred on the Calton Hill. The western development followed only a couple of years later. Shandwick Place is its southern thoroughfare, as Princes Street is of the original New Town: it is flanked by a matching pair of curved crescents in classical style, Coates Crescent to the north and **Atholl Crescent** to the south. The line of Shandwick Place is continued south-west by West Maitland Street as far as the Haymarket, no more a market now than the Grassmarket and Lawnmarket in the Old Town. **Haymarket Station**, built in 1840–2 at the height of Edinburgh's railway fever, was the original terminus of the line from Glasgow before it was extended eastwards to Waverley, and retains something of its early Victorian appearance.

Haymarket Terrace, leading west, presently reveals on its north side the extraordinary outline of **Donaldson's School**, one of Playfair's last buildings (1842–51). Like his New College above the Mound, it is very far from his Neoclassical norm; this time he aimed at an elaborate (some would say over-elaborate) approximation of the manner of Inigo Jones. It clearly owes much to George Heriot's Hospital, a product of that period, and may also remind English visitors of Burghley House near Stamford in Lincolnshire. It is certainly impressive, seen to spectacular advantage in its large grounds – another of those Edinburgh buildings that always seem not quite real, endowing the city with touches of pure fairy-tale.

Queensferry Street, leading north-west from the West End at right angles to Shandwick Place, gives access on its left to **Melville Street**, the grand central thoroughfare of the Western New Town. Designed in 1814, this is the George Street of the western development, broadened and varied by a spacious central circus with a statue of Robert Dundas, the second Lord Melville. At its western end, dominating the skyline, towers George Gilbert Scott's Gothic **St Mary's Cathedral**, the second largest church in Scotland and centre of the Scottish Episcopalian Diocese of Edinburgh. It was largely endowed by Mary and Barbara, the daughters of a wealthy Edinburgh attorney, William Walker; they stipulated that the church should carry the name of their mother, Mary. The small twin spires in front of the 200-foot central one are known as the 'Mary' and 'Barbara' spires.

Queensferry Street itself follows the old coaching route towards Queensferry and the Forth Bridges; in a surprisingly short time full urban development gives

56 *The Scottish American War Memorial in West Princes Street Gardens.*

way to the pleasant and still thickly wooded valley of the Water of Leith, a 20-mile trout stream that flows from the Pentland Hills to the Firth of Forth, which it enters at Edinburgh's seaport. At one time it powered over 70 mills. The road crosses the steep-sided valley along the 100-foot high **Dean Bridge**, a graceful feat of engineering by Thomas Telford (**59**). Its construction in 1832 overcame the main geographical barrier to further north-westward expansion of the city. From the bridge the visitor can look down on the delightful old **Dean Village** (**60**) by the waterside and on the Doric rotunda (another Claude-like conceit) that marks **St Bernard's Well**, a mineral spring whose water – so one authority declared in 1805 – 'has a slight resemblance in flavour to the washings of a foul gun barrel'. To the west of Trinity Church at the north end of the bridge lies the **Dean Cemetery**, maybe the richest of all the memorial-rich Edinburgh burial grounds. Playfair himself is buried here, with his own monument, not far as the crow flies from Donaldson's School, which many of his contemporaries thought his masterpiece. Here too are Francis Jeffrey, the classicist John Stewart Blackie, and Sir Hector Macdonald VC – 'Fighting Mac', the most admired of Scotland's Victorian soldiers, whose suicide at the peak of his career, after being accused of a homosexual offence, caused a national sensation.

Queensferry Road continues west towards the city outskirts, passing the turreted **Daniel Stewart's College**, contemporary with Donaldson's School, and like it set massively in its own grounds and much influenced by George Heriot's Hospital. The architect was David Rhind. A little to the south, roughly equidistant between these two neo-Renaissance schools, is a severely classical

one – the **Scottish Museum of Modern Art**, opened to the public during the 1984 Festival but designed by William Burn as John Watson's School. An exact contemporary of the Royal High School on Calton Hill, Burn's design is much plainer and simpler, a single long Palladian block with a prominent Doric portico. It is the only public gallery in Britain devoted entirely to 20th-century art. The collection, which in Britain is second only to that of the Tate Gallery in London, was originally opened in 1960 in Inverleith House (see below, p. 85) and is especially strong in Expressionist art. Cézanne, Epstein, Gaudier-Brzeska, Giacometti, Barbara Hepworth, Gwen John, Kandinsky, Klee, Kokoschka, L. S. Lowry, Matisse, Mondrian, Henry Moore, Nolde, Picasso, Sickert, and Graham Sutherland are all well represented, as are many contemporary Scottish artists, such as Robin Philipson and Ann Redpath.

The Moray Estate and Northern New Town

In 1803, before either the Eastern or Western New Towns were begun, a **Northern New Town** had started to spread downhill northwards from Queen Street Gardens onto land previously owned by George Heriot's Hospital and the Earl of Moray. **Randolph Crescent**, south of the Dean Bridge off Queensferry Street, leads into the latest, but also probably the best part of the northern development, the **Moray Estate**. Begun in 1822, the Estate is a self-contained and highly imaginative piece of town planning executed under stringent conditions, laid down by the Earl himself, by James Gillespie Graham of Orchil, a flamboyant and ambitious architect who enjoyed the Earl's patronage and

59 *Thomas Telford's elegant Dean Bridge, carrying the main road to Queensferry, was provided by a private speculator, Lord Provost Learmouth, who had purchased the land and building rights on the north bank of the Water of Leith at this point.*

confidence. Graham had a difficult sloping site to work with, hemmed in between the Water of Leith and Craig's New Town, but he rose to the challenge superbly, proving himself another of Edinburgh's architectural geniuses. Essentially the Estate is a sequence of crescent, oval, and polygon, parallel with the river valley and at 45 degrees to the north-western corner of the New Town, which the oval, **Ainslie Place**, just shaves. The scale of the streets and places is grand, but not oppressive, and each geometrical expanse is enlivened by wooded gardens. The crown of the conception is the sumptuous **Moray Place** (**61**), a twelve-sided circus. The Earl lived at No. 28, enjoying the scenic advantages of a development to which he had contributed not a penny apart from some legal fees and Graham's commission: all the buildings and amenities had to be funded by the feuars themselves.

From Moray Place, Darnaway Street leads east into **Heriot Row**, the severely grand southern avenue of the Northern New Town proper (R. L. Stevenson spent most of his life at No. 17). Robert Reid and William Sibbald, who provided the original plan for this development in 1801–2, took several leaves from James Craig's book. 'Their' New Town, like his and like the later Western New Town, is largely a matter of parallel thoroughfares, the central one (in this case Great King Street) linking two large open spaces. But the thoroughfares are more numerous, and as they march northwards they become progressively less monumental, while the concepts of the curve and the circle, apparently unknown to Craig but made necessary here by the contours of the site, add frequent and welcome variety. **Abercomby Place**, the eastward

60 Dean Village, huddled beside the Water of Leith, is five minutes' walk from the centre of the New Town. The river powered the meal-mills which were the village's livelihood; now the mill and granary buildings, some dating from the 17th century, have largely been restored as offices and blocks of flats.

extension of Heriot Row and like it bounded on the south by Queen Street Gardens, was the first curved street in Edinburgh, the shallowness of its curve creating a vista of remarkable length. Great King Street runs between **Royal Circus** (**62**), in the west (by Playfair), and **Drummond Place** in the east (by Robert Reid). It is fitting that this pleasant, garden-filled 'square' (the eastern side is a curve) should bear the name of Lord Provost Drummond, who had dreamed of such grand civic development in the previous century: 'Great Drummond improveth what nature doth send; / To country and city he's always a friend' (James Wilson, 1760).

North-east of Royal Circus in St Stephen Street is one of Playfair's most ingenious buildings, **St Stephen's Church**, (1827). The interior is octagonal, but the outside is diamond-shaped; Doric peristyles carry a gallery along each side, and a square-section campanile is set upon the south-facing end, its yawning portal like an open mouth at the foot of the street's downward slope.

The Northern New Town dissipates itself northwards to end in an area of unpretentious housing erected in mid-Victorian times alongside the Water of Leith, which at this point runs almost west–east. On its east side it is bounded by the line of Broughton Street and **Bellevue Crescent**, another long shallow crescent, planned as early as 1802 and with the further refinement of being stepped on a descending slope. At the centre of its arc stands **St Mary's Church**, built in 1826 to an elegantly proportioned design by Thomas Brown. Above a large Ionic portico rises a tall, slim, circular spire with two tiers of surrounding peristyles and a small elongated dome. The effect is rather Florentine.

61 *Two of the twelve sides of Moray Place.*

62 *A section of Royal Circus, the western end of the Northern New Town, showing the elegant curve of its circumference.*

Further north, at the north-eastern corner of the area, a road bridge crosses the river to the district of Inverleith, where Edinburgh's **Royal Botanic Gardens** (**63**) are situated. The city has possessed a Botanic Garden since at least 1670, but the present site has only been occupied from the 1820s. It covers some 70 acres of rolling ground just north of the river, and is one of the most important institutions of its kind in the British Isles. An enormous diversity of trees, shrubs, and flowering plants are displayed, many of them grown from specimens discovered by Scottish collectors on expeditions all over the world. Its primary function is the advancement of botanical knowledge and the training of gardeners and foresters, but over the past century it has also been one of the city's most popular parks. Its outdoor rock garden, established by Isaac Balfour, the Regius Keeper in the 1890s, has a particularly extensive collection of Alpine specimens and is world famous. There are huge indoor collections of exotic plants in the Palm House, a splendid Victorian construction of cast iron and glass, and in the modern Arboretum New Glass Houses. The monumental Herbarium, opened in 1964, contains a major horticultural library and a collection of over two million species in a building of almost Mediterranean aspect, with arched windows and graceful white terrazzo facing.

Behind the Glass Houses is a memorial to the great Danish botanist Linnaeus, pioneer of species classification, by Robert Adam; and at the southern end of the Gardens, at the highest point, is **Inverleith House**, a fine Georgian mansion which was for long the residence of the Regius Keeper and from 1960 to 1984 housed the then Scottish National Gallery of Modern Art.

West of the Botanic Gardens lies **Inverleith Park**, one of the city's largest recreational areas and especially notable for its huge lozenge-shaped pond (popular with model boat enthusiasts). Still further west stands a building that, in a city of imposing schools, must rank among the most splendid – **Fettes College** (1862–70), designed by David Bryce, who was original enough to look neither to ancient Greece nor to the example of George Heriot's Hospital, but rather to French châteaux of the period of Louis XIV. Edinburgh's architectural fantasies can hardly go further than this translation of the glories of Blois or Chenonceaux, massed into an outline of near-perfect symmetry which is the more flamboyant and impressive for being set against the northern skyline, where it has no rival. The long list of distinguished former pupils includes the composer Michael Tippett.

By the mid-1820s Edinburgh was expanding rapidly and grandiosely to west, north, and east: it must have seemed to many contemporaries that the process could be indefinite. In fact, plain economics were against it, though the city fathers seem to have taken great pains to conceal plain economics from themselves for as long as they could. Even though the supplementary New Towns were largely private ventures, the city Council was heavily involved financially.

63 *A typical corner of the Botanic Gardens.*

It has been calculated (long after the event) that something like a third of its annual income was being spent on building projects alone. Yet Edinburgh's finances had been in disarray since the turn of the century – to the extent that, by the 1820s, there was no one on the Council who properly understood them. Finally all came to grief over yet another ambitious project, the extension of Leith Docks, which involved the Council in heavy borrowing from the Government: in 1833 the city was discovered to be bankrupt to the tune of £400,000, and the era of the planned New Towns came to an end, though isolated public buildings and private developments continued to be put up.

Another significant force for change was the arrival of the railways, which started in 1831 with the opening of a local line from St Leonards on the south-eastern outskirts of the city to the nearby town of Dalkeith. An Edinburgh, Leith, and Newhaven Railway was incorporated in 1836, and the line from Glasgow to Haymarket was opened in 1842. Very soon there was a proposal to extend both these systems to meet at the new **Waverley Station**, which was in operation by 1846, situated under North Bridge between the Old and New Towns. As already mentioned, the Glasgow line was cut directly through Princes Street Gardens. The line from Newhaven, being led round the northern and eastern sides of the Calton Hill to approach Waverley from the opposite direction, put the final stop to the advance of the Eastern New Town.

That development ends with the northern side of the section of London Road between Leith Walk and Easter Road – **Leopold Place** and **Hillside Crescent** – and the southernmost portion of Leith Walk itself, known as **Elm Row** (the name commemorates a fine double row of elm trees, nearly 200 yards long, which stood here well into the 19th century). These buildings are by Playfair, as are the terraces above London Road Gardens, and they are good standard work from him – the monumental pillars on the curved four-storey corners of Leopold Place and **Windsor Street** are especially striking, and the rooms within those corners are of shapes unknown to simple geometry. On the western side of Leith Walk is **Gayfield Square**, an earlier, independent development of 1791 centred on a beautiful little three-storey Georgian mansion that was already built – as a country house – in 1763. Less celebrated than more pompous New Town developments, the square is a gem, and affords a fine view of the Calton Hill.

In 1970, with Government support and perhaps alerted by the loss of St James' Square and much of York Place, the Edinburgh City Council and the Historic Buildings Council began work on a conservation programme embracing the whole of the New Town. As a result this large area of virtually intact Georgian development is now a priority conservation site protected by stringent planning controls.

4 Places to Visit near Edinburgh

Leith Street and Leith Walk lead from Princes Street all the way to the busy seaport of **Leith**, with its large deep-water harbour and docks. There has been settlement in the area around the outflow of the Water of Leith for over 800 years, and the harbour has been commercially important since Edward I captured Berwick for England in 1296. Amalgamation with Edinburgh only took place in 1920. The Church of St Mary's, Kirkgate, by Thomas Hamilton, contains parts of an older 15th-century church. Andro Lamb's house (now restored as an old people's Day Centre) is a well-preserved Renaissance house of Scots-Hanseatic pattern, and was the home of the merchant with whom Mary, Queen of Scots stayed her first night in Scotland on her return from France in 1561. The grand Exchange building of 1809, the Customs House (1812) in palatial Doric, and the Old Town Hall (1828) are as impressive as contemporary buildings in the New Town. Trinity House (1816), a charitable institution for Leith's merchant seamen, incorporates a foundation that goes back to 1380.

Leith Links nearby has a hallowed significance for golfers, though it is now a public park rather than a golf-course. The game – one of Scotland's many cultural gifts to the world – originated in the Middle Ages, and must have been widely popular by 1457, when King James II tried to encourage his soldiers to more warlike relaxations by decreeing that 'Fute-ball and Golfe be utterly cryed down'. Clearly he was unsuccessful, and in 1593 Leith Links was recognized as the world's first official golf-course, with a grand total of five holes. Charles I is said to have been playing golf on the Links when he received the news of the Irish Rebellion in 1641; and it was here, in 1744, that the first rules of the game were drawn up. Two artificial mounds on the Links, known as Giant's Brae and Lady Fife's Brae, are relics of gun emplacements constructed by the English when they besieged Leith in 1560.

The Forth coastline is well worth exploring: to the west of Leith there are fishing villages, country walks, and country houses; to the east is the Georgian seaside resort of **Portobello**, a suburb fashionable as a watering-place since the 18th century, with a sandy beach and two miles of promenade. The Police Station is a Victorian imitation castle; the battlemented Portobello Tower at the promenade's western end is one of the oldest buildings, incorporating medieval fragments of demolished houses from the Royal Mile; and the Art Nouveau spires of St John's Catholic Church (1903) send a faint incongruous echo of Gaudí's Barcelona across the skyline.

Further east lie the seaside village of **Joppa**; **Musselburgh** town on the River

64 *The 15th-century Rosslyn Chapel, with its famous 'Prentice Pillar'.*

Esk, famous for its race-course and golf facilities; **Prestonpans**, which supported an oyster fishery until the last century; and **Port Seton**, dominated by a vast modern power station but also graced by **Seton House**, designed by Robert Adam in 1790. The splendid **Brunstane House**, inland from Joppa on Brunstane Road North, dates from the 16th century and was rebuilt in 1639 for the Duke of Lauderdale. Its interiors are notable for plasterwork by William Adam, father of Robert.

Between Leith and Portobello but inland towards Holyrood Park and Meadowbank is **Restalrig Church**, an ancient monument which used to be the main church for Leith. Much of it was destroyed in the late 16th century as a 'Monument of Idolatrie', but beneath the 19th-century restorations (by William Burn) the remarkable 'St Triduana's Well', a vaulted hexagonal aisle of the 15th century, remains intact.

Westward of Leith lie the fishing villages of **Newhaven** and **Granton**. Newhaven, founded by James IV about 1500, was the building place of his huge warship *The Great Michael* – Scotland's equivalent of the *Mary Rose* – whose construction reputedly consumed all the trees in Fife. Granton boasts Caroline Park, an unexpectedly grand mansion of the late 17th century with unusual ogival-roofed towers, sadly overshadowed by gasworks and industrial detritus.

Slightly inland and to the west of Granton, overlooking the Firth of Forth, is **Lauriston Castle** (**65**), a late-16th-century tower-house to which neo-Jacobean additions were made in the early 19th century. Once it was the home

65 *Lauriston Castle: the original 16th-century T-shaped tower (left) was built by Archibald Napier, father of the mathematician. A later owner, John Law (1671–1729), founded the first Bank in France and obtained sole trading rights in the vast area of the Lower Mississippi which he christened Louisiana in honour of the French king. The house was much extended in neo-Jacobean style by William Burn in the early 19th century.*

of John Law, the Scots financier to Louis XIV of France. The Castle is preserved as an Edwardian country mansion, open to the public, with period furniture and a collection of *objets d'art*.

On the coastline itself, **Silverknowes** promenade and golf-course provide a pleasant shore-and-country walk westward to the picturesque village of **Cramond**, a popular yachting centre on the estuary of the River Almond. Extensive Roman remains of the 2nd century have been excavated here; the village itself is mainly 18th-century industrial. There is also a 17th-century church, the 16th-century Old Cramond Brig or Bridge (where King James V, travelling incognito as was his custom, is said to have been attacked by robbers), and the recently restored Cramond Tower, a medieval foundation of the Bishops of Dunkeld, which may have been part of a now vanished castle. There is a beautiful wooded walk southward up the banks of the Almond.

A local ferry service still crosses the Almond at Cramond; about two miles west stands **Dalmeny House** (1815) by William Wilkins, home of the Earls of Rosebery, a pleasing essay in Tudor Gothic (**66**). The small 12th-century church in **Dalmeny** village, further west and just inland from Queensferry, has a richly carved south doorway and a beautiful semi-circular vaulted apse – an outstanding example of the Romanesque style in Scotland.

Queensferry itself is an ancient place (the queen celebrated in its name is the 11th-century St Margaret) and owes its importance to its position at a point where the Firth narrows, almost opposite the royal town of Dunfermline in Fife, which was Scotland's capital long before Edinburgh. Queensferry became a royal burgh before 1641: among its important buildings are the 17th-century

Plewlands House, the medieval Priory Church of St Mary of Carmel, and the Hawes Inn, which features in R. L. Stevenson's *Kidnapped*. The little harbour, busy until the 1960s when the Forth Road Bridge finally made the car ferry redundant, provides a good vantage-point for the hills of Fife, the islands of the Forth (the Isle of May is a bird-reserve), the naval base at Rosyth, and the two **Forth Bridges** that link Edinburgh with the Scottish Highlands. The immense steel cantilevered Railway Bridge (1883–90), over a mile and a half long and 360 feet high, incorporating 60,000 tons of steel and 10,000,000 rivets, is a staggering monument to Victorian engineering and three-dimensional geometry (**67**); beside it the slim suspension bridge that carries the road link, opened in 1964, seems almost frail, yet it is one of the largest in the world, its steel cables carrying a 3,300-foot central span (**68**). It is open to pedestrians and affords memorable views of the Rail Bridge and the Firth.

Two miles further west from Queensferry, near the shore of the Firth, is **Hopetoun House** (**69**), renowned as the finest Adam mansion in Scotland. Home of the Marchioness of Linlithgow, it houses a large collection of art treasures and is open to the public, as are its 100 acres of gardens and deer parks.

Directly south of Queensferry, at a bend in the River Almond, stands **Kirkliston**. Here the parish church, dedicated in 1244 to a saint whose name has been forgotten, is a particularly interesting example of the transition between Norman and Early English architecture (as in the west tower, with its saddle-back roof), and it was well restored and added to in the 19th century. Further up the Almond is the countryside park of Almondell.

67 *The Forth Railway Bridge – until 1964 'the' Forth Bridge – seen from South Queensferry. The most impressive view of it is from the waters of the Firth itself, but the demise of the car-ferry has made this less available than it used to be. Despite its skeletal structure the bridge presents 135 acres of steel to wind and weather, and requires continuous repainting.*

On the return to Edinburgh from Kirkliston the main Edinburgh–Glasgow road passes, to the north, the **Scottish National Zoological Park** on the sheltered southern slopes of Corstorphine Hills. By far the largest zoo in Scotland, it covers 80 acres and has been a major attraction for visitors since it was opened in 1914. It has large collections of mammals, reptiles, birds, fish, and arthropods, but is famous above all for its penguins (**70**) – the largest breeding colony of Antarctic penguins anywhere outside Antarctica itself. High on the list of other attractions are the polar bears and sea-lions in their specially landscaped environments, the rare Père David's Deer, the Tropical Bird House, Parrot Garden, and Children's Farm.

The Corstorphine area was once an outlying village. Near the Zoo but on the south of the main road is **Corstorphine Church**, dating from the early 15th century, with picturesque gabled roofs. The nearby Dovecot, pierced by over a thousand pigeon holes, is all that remains of a 16th-century castle.

To the south of the city lie the residential suburbs of Merchiston, Marchmont, Newington, and Morningside, all once villages in their own right. **Marchmont** used to boast a select girls' school named after St Trinnean, from which the cartoonist Ronald Searle derived the idea for his famous horrendous public school, St Trinian's. In the centre of Merchiston is **Merchiston Tower**, a gaunt 15th-century tower-house which was the home of the great mathematician John Napier and is now the nexus of the modern **Napier College**, named in his honour and constructed in the 1960s as a technical college with facilities for 4,000 students. Beyond Morningside – traditionally Edinburgh's élite

68 *The Forth Road Bridge was the largest suspension bridge in Europe when opened by Queen Elizabeth II. It cost £20,000,000 to build and, together with its approach viaducts (one of which is visible on the left) carries two dual carriageways and two pedestrian walkways a distance of over a mile and a half.*

69 *Robert Adam, his father William, and his brother John were all involved in the design and decoration of the sumptuous Hopetoun House (1699–1751), whose large flanking wings give it the extraordinarily broad front seen in this view. In recent years it has become a popular venue for occasional concerts of Baroque music.*

70 *A few handsome individuals from Edinburgh Zoo's world-famous colony of penguins.*

suburb, renowned for a local accent of 'rifained' sensitivity – Comiston Road leads southwards past **Blackford Hill**, with its Royal Observatory, and the **Braid Hills**. Across their slopes sweeps a portion of the great ring of golf-courses that practically encircles Edinburgh from Cramond to Duddingston; and beyond them lie the greater and imperishably romantic **Pentland Hills**, the city's southern defence and, over the ages, a paradisal refuge for its leading spirits. Here in **Swanston** village, an 18th-century huddle of whitewashed cottages, is the summer home of R. L. Stevenson, who found in the area around Glencorse, a few miles away, the brooding landscapes of his unfinished master-piece *Weir of Hermiston*. A little to the west of Swanston stands the aristocratic yet homely **Bonaly Tower**, built by Playfair as the beloved retreat of Lord Cock-burn from his metropolitan cares as Solicitor-General for Scotland.

By contrast the south-eastern road beyond Newington, the Old Dalkeith Road, passes the splendid ruins of **Craigmillar Castle**, a roofless but otherwise extremely well preserved medieval fortress. It was begun in 1374 in the reign of King Robert II, founder of the Stewart dynasty, and was favoured by several rulers of his line; Queen Mary withdrew here in 1566 for solace after the murder of Rizzio at Holyrood. Roslin Village, five miles further along the road, also contains a castle and still more important, the exquisite **Rosslyn Chapel** (**64**), founded in 1446. The interior is profusely decorated with beautiful 15th-century carving that shows Continental influence, and the *pièce de résistance* is the elaborate foliage that adorns the 'Prentice Pillar', reputedly the work of an ambitious stone-mason's apprentice seeking to outdo his master. The chapel is occasionally used for concerts, especially at Festival time; to hear early music, by a composer such as Dufay, performed in this contemporary setting is an unforgettable experience.